KIZZIE
DEFYING THE ODDS

KIZZIE L. CRAWFORD, MBA

KIZZIE DEFYING THE ODDS

By

Kizzie L. Crawford, MBA

Foreword:

Dr. Pauline E. Wallner, DM, MBA, CPM

Published by

Kizzie L. Crawford

www.authorkizziecrawford.com

www.linkktr.ee/kizziethecloser

All rights reserved. No part of this electronic or printed book may be duplicated or transferred in any form or means, electronic or manual, including photocopying, recording, or any data storage or retrieval system without explicit, written permission from the author, except for brief citation in a review.

Copyright © 2023 Author Kizzie L. Crawford
ISBN: 9798859671397
Printed in the United States of America

TABLE OF CONTENTS

DEDICATION

ACKNOWLEDGMENTS

FOREWORD

PROLOGUE

CHAPTER 1

CHAPTER 2

CHAPTER 3

CHAPTER 5

CHAPTER 6

CHAPTER 7

CHAPTER 8

CHAPTER 9

CHAPTER 10

CHAPTER 11

CHAPTER 12

CHAPTER 13

CHAPTER 16

CHAPTER 17

CHAPTER 18

EPILOGUE

DEDICATION

I dedicate this book to my mother, my husband my children, my extended family, my village of friends, and everyone who has impacted my life along the way either through assistance, prayer or encouragement.

KIZZIE CRAWFORD

ACKNOWLEDGMENTS

I would like to acknowledge my husband who allows me to be who I am unapologetically. He supports me in everything that I do regardless of what it is and he encourages me to be better than I was last week and last year. We are totally different in most things but when it comes to love, support, family, business and building a legacy we go together like peanut butter and jelly.

I would like to acknowledge my son Thomas a/k/a King who has always been my motivation even before he was born. His presence always pushed me to be a better person so that I could provide the life for him that I wish I had. He motivates me daily by telling me how proud he is of me and how he appreciates all the sacrifices that I have made to provide a great life for him.

I would like to acknowledge my mom for always being my biggest cheerleader over the years. She worked extremely hard while I was growing up to provide all that she could for us.

She took a lot of mistreatments just to give us a better life. Those things will never go unnoticed by me. I know her life would have been completely different if she wouldn't have had to support us, but she decided to always be there even when it was hard.

I would like to acknowledge my Uncle Larry for pushing me to write this book even when I didn't want to. He read my drafts and gave me feedback over the last year in a half.

He would send me random text messages to ask me how far I was on the book. If it wasn't for him, you might not be reading this book right now. Thank you, Uncle Larry, for your help.

I would like to thank Dr. Pauline E. Wallner who was willing to jump in to assist me as soon as she found out that I was writing a book and needed assistance with self-publishing it.

She read my manuscript, introduced me to self-publishing it and was willing to write a Forward for my book that almost brought me to tears.

Finally, I would like to acknowledge my grandmother Almarie. My grandmother always wanted the best for her family and always did whatever she could to support us in whatever we needed.

We had an extremely close relationship and a bond that was unbreakable. She taught me so many things and I took a lot of ways after her. She died of Cancer years ago and I miss her dearly.

I'm glad I was able to be with her during her illness and show her how much I loved her. I wish she was here to see me now. I know she would be so proud.

FOREWORD

When Kizzie Crawford posted a question on Meta (Facebook), asking her followers if they would purchase a book she authored, I answered immediately with a resounding "Yes."

You see, I knew what it was like to have a story penned in my brain for several years just waiting for the right moment to share it with the world. I knew then that I wanted to play a role in Kizzie Crawford's debut as a published author.

She was already my real estate coach at Keller Williams Realty Atlanta Partners, and continue to gift her mentoring skills to the men and women who have dual careers.

I pray that you too will say "Yes" to this book of an incredible story of faith over fear, triumph over adversity, and resilience beyond measure.

I met Kizzie Crawford a little over a year ago and became immediately fascinated with the tenacity, real estate expertise, and collaboration competencies she demonstrated.

Not only is she an accomplished real estate professional, but she also inspires her mentees to reframe, refocus, and recharge the overarching three letter question: "Why?" She epitomizes the Keller creed:

"Don't let small thinking cut your life down to size. Think big, aim high, act bold. And see just how big you can blow up your life" (Gary Keller).

This brings me to the purpose of this forward which is to provide a synopsis of Kizzie Crawford's "Whys?" When we observe the life of a successful entrepreneur, it is easy to assume that their success is overnight.

What we rarely address is the journey fraught with hills and valleys, joy and pain, love and loss, and failure or success.

In my humble Jamaican family culture, we would describe it as a "Hill and Gully" ride. To borrow Alicia Keys' musical lyrics: **"This girl is on fire"** and she is not afraid to take calculated risks and bold moves.

Stories told are lessons learned to let others know that they are not alone. Every story in this book has a lesson for someone. Effective leaders, a well-earned ascription for Kizzie Crawford, understand the power of vulnerability.

For example, if you have never been homeless, you may find it difficult to relate to someone struggling to find stability through homeownership.

If you have not experienced a parent, family, or friend struggling with the aftermath and choices when substance abuse grabs ahold of all the senses, you may not truly understand when the American dream turns to tragedy.

Through her stories and coaching Kizzie

Crawford's strategy is to introduce homeownership to first-time homebuyers and to assist existing homeowners to design the next steps.

An important aspect of her community outreach is the non-for-profit initiative with Distinguished Young Ladies, the true essence of a grass roots seed-planter.

In other words, by reading the content of this book, a clear line of sight was realized as Kizzie Crawford's "Why?" unfold in each chapter and line.

The stories include visits of an innocent child to a father in prison; the trauma of addiction and broken promises; the drama and toxicity that sometimes manifest in blended families; longing for deployed family in the military during a tumultuous period; volatile middle school experience, and the decision to fail fast and early in various career pursuits.

These can be described as formative years where territorial fights evolve and right emerges from the ashes of a sidewalk teenage brawl, and where familial cohesion and love stick like glue one hot afternoon.

Despite all the ways that Kizzie Crawford's life could have been different, she chose the beautiful parts of her life's journey to carve a path for her success.

She carries a light that masks her experiences and yet, a brilliant level of emotional intelligence that allows her to communicate effectively with people from diverse cultures and backgrounds.

Rather than complain about her past or current situations that may not be serving her well, she finds a way to reframe her thinking and thrive.

As you dive deeper into Kizzie Crawford's stories, you will realize that she boldly embraces risks with courage and resilience.

> ***"You gain strength, courage, and confidence by every experience in which you really stop to look fear in the face. You must do the thing you think you cannot do." (Eleanor Roosevelt).***

Leaders who have a love for people reflect on the human condition. They tend to appreciate, recognize, and empathize with the struggles of others. In so doing, they build internal strengths that shine no matter how bleak or dark their reality.

> ***"A genuine leader is not a searcher for consensus but a molder of consensus" (Martin Luther King, Jr.).***

In 2019, I pledged wholeheartedly to do what so many others, including Dr. Michael B. Grossman, had done for me with my memoir, Rising Stronger: Living, Loving, and Leading from a Seat of Gratitude.

Subsequently, I coauthored a book titled: Loving and Essential Paths to Healing After Losing a Child. The third book in the Rising Stronger Series: Finding Balance During Perpetual Storms was written and published during the covid shutdown.

Nothing brought me more peace than penning my memoir and sharing my life experience so that others can truly overcome stumbling blocks and inevitable storms.

It is my greatest honor to pass the torch to my coach and mentor in the real estate industry, Kizzie Crawford. May your continued search for meaning and purpose bring honor to God and your fellowman.

I do look forward to a series of books as you expand your horizon and join the global speaker's path. I strongly recommend this book to all who wish to learn, share, and grow.

Keep Rising Stronger!

> **Dr. Pauline E. Wallner, DM, AMA-CPM, MBA, BSc, Finance**

KIZZIE CRAWFORD

PROLOGUE

When I was seventeen and a senior in college, I thought I had my life mapped out perfectly. I was convinced that I would enter the Navy and they would fund my college education.

I was engaged and had plans to marry my high school sweetheart immediately after I graduated with the goal of him following me to my duty stations in California.

I dreamed of the military paying for my law degree, and I felt that would be the beginning of a beautiful life and the end of any finanical worries. Looking back, it's funny how we believe we know it all at that age, but truthfully, we hardly knew anything at all.

KIZZIE CRAWFORD

CHAPTER 1

My name is Kizzie Lashaun and anyone who ever saw the movie *Roots*, has heard the name Kizzie before. I originally was going to be named Jessica, but my grandmother Almarie asked my mom what she thought of that name Kizzie.

My mom loved the name and because it was unique, she agreed. The movie came out in 1977, and my mom was pregnant with me when she watched it. One definition of my name is Stay Put which is the total opposite of who I am, and you'll see that as the book goes on. But I do love the uniqueness of my name.

If you hear of anyone else named Kizzie, trust and believe, they were probably born after 1997. People love to ask me if it is a nickname or short for something, and I say no. Kizzie is my real name, and I'm so glad my grandmother mentioned it.

I was born and raised in a small town called Adel, Georgia. When I say small, I mean small. The population is around 5500 people, it has two elementary schools, one middle school, and one high school.

Everyone knows everyone in Adel for the most part. This can be a good thing, but it can also be bad. You cannot go to the store without seeing someone you know. You couldn't get away with anything because people were always looking and talking.

I remember walking to school one time when I shouldn't have and my mom found out about it before I made it back home. I'll give more details of that story later. Adel wasn't known for a lot but it was well known for The King Frog and Cook County Ford, who coined the slogan "That's Adel Baby."

My parents were teenage parents, and I was the second of the two kids they had together. I have an older brother, who is named Vanico Devane, but we call him Nico for short. He is fifteen months older than me.

With that being said, we definitely were not planned. My mom Jeanette, Nette is her nickname for family and friends, and my dad Devane, but everyone calls him Bane for short, knew and liked each other at the early age of eleven. They didn't get serious and call themselves dating until they were about sixteen.

My mom got pregnant at sixteen and had my brother nine days after she turned seventeen. She got pregnant about eight months later and had me in May of 1978, which was Mother's Day. I guess you can say Nico was her birthday present, and I was her Mother's Day present.

Neither of my parents were from wealthy families, so you can imagine times were tough for my mom. My grandparents helped as well. When my brother was born, my Grandmother Almarie and Grandaddy B kept my brother for a while to help my mom and dad finish school.

But unfortunately, my grandfather got sick, and my mom and dad had to take care of my brother full time. Then I came along. That really ended the school career even though they both were so close to finishing.

Both of my parents dropped out of school and never returned to get their degrees. I would love to see my mom get her degree. I hate that because of us she couldn't finish and get a better paying job. She always worked at jobs that did not pay a lot of money. Because of this, she did everything in her power to encourage and push us to finish high school.

My mom's dad, Grandaddy Tom, was furious when my mom got pregnant. He was not the most supportive parent then and took the news hard. He had such high hopes for his baby girl and because of this, he took his anger out on her.

This was another reason my father's parents helped so much and volunteered to keep Nico. But eventually, my maternal grandparents came around and helped her with babysitting and medical bills.

When my mom found out that she was pregnant with me, she wanted to get married, because she didn't want to have two kids out of wedlock. So, they both went to the courthouse to get married.

My mom was not eighteen at this time, so my grandfather had to agree and sign off on her getting married. We lived together as one big, not-so-happy family for probably a year before my mom left my dad. My dad changed after my mom got pregnant. He was the best thing ever before then but once the babies came everything changed.

It got even worse when she got pregnant with me. While she was pregnant, he would leave her alone to take care of my brother and ran the streets with other women with no regard to my mom's feelings. He literally hit my mom in the stomach while she was pregnant with me to make her lose me.

He never wanted me and wanted her to abort me but because she didn't agree, he tried to take matters in his own hands. Can you imagine how I felt when I learned this as an adult. It definitely didn't make me feel all nice and fuzzy inside. My mom finally had enough of the cheating, physical abuse, and disrespect, and we left.

That was the best thing she could have done. Our life would have been a living hell if she had stayed. I don't know how our life would have turned out if we had been exposed to my dad living in the home with us day in and day out.

It would have been tough seeing the disrespect that he showed my mom on a daily basis. Most kids want their parents to stay together and if they divorce, pray that they get back together. We NEVER prayed that prayer.

We lived with Grandma Gloria and Granddaddy Tom on and off over the years. It wasn't the most comfortable living arrangement because my mom's younger siblings also lived there, but we all made it work. It seemed like we all grew up together including my mom, because she was so young when she had us.

My mom worked two jobs to take care of us over the years. My dad was never a real provider for us when my mom and dad were together for that short time. He actually lost his job the day they got married.

Soon after my mom left, my dad was imprisoned for armed robbery and sentenced to around seven years. He had previously been to jail for minor theft, but jail wasn't an option this time. It was prison time.

This left my mom to take care of two kids with no financial support from our father at all, not that he was helping prior to that. She was working at Talley's, a sawmill, and as a maid at The King Frog Motel.

Grandma Almarie and Grandaddy B would help out a lot by buying us clothes and Christmas presents. They really tried to take some of the slack off Mom since our dad was not around.

They would also take us to the prison to see our dad when we were young. I remember one time we went to see him. It was myself, Nico, Grandma Almarie, and Grandaddy B. I remember being so young, maybe three or four, and that I didn't want to sit still.

I kept moving around and playing under the table. Boy, when Grandma got a hold of me, I promise you I learned to sit still. She was one of those old-school grandparents that will get you wherever you act up. She didn't play that "Wait until you get home".

I remember looking at the picture of the visit and noticed I was wearing a pair of pink cowboy boots, and Nico had brown ones. I have no idea why. I want to think that was one of the only times, or at least the last time, that I went to see my dad while he was serving his 7-year prison term. I don't recall too much more about those visits.

When I became an adult, I visited my dad during one of his prison stints in a near by city. However, this was not a life I wanted to continue having, so that was the last time I visited him.

We grew up moving place to place. Several of those places included the Projects, and some of those we lived repeatedly. In Adel, there are two different Projects, and we lived in both.

One was near a sawmill factory called Del-Cook which most people call the "Black Folks" Projects because it's in the black neighborhood. They were block apartments that were attached like duplexes. We shared a porch with the neighbor. I used to love to stand outside and pump my arm up and down to get the truck drivers to pull the string to honk their horns. It never got too old for me.

My mom started dating a man who eventually became my stepdad while we were staying there. His name was Robert but we called him Rob. We tried calling him dad after they got married, but we kept calling him Rob so eventually, he told us to stop trying and just call him Rob.

I'm not sure if it hurt his feelings that we couldn't remember to call him dad or if he was just tired of us trying. Truth is, I wanted to call him dad because he eventually became the only dad I had a relationship with.

Rob worked at Del-Cook, and I would stand outside on the porch waiting for him to get off. I always liked Rob, and we got along well when I was young. However, he was very strict, which caused us to get a lot of whippings.

Before I go any further, let me just say, this is not a case of child abuse. However, we grew up in a time where people believed in disciplining their children with whippings. I know some people don't believe in whippings and think kids shouldn't be punished that way, and I can see their point.

However, I never felt that mom and Rob were bad parents because of it. I appreciate the discipline I received as a child because I swear some of the adults I see with no home raising, should have gotten whippings or something. So now back to my story.

He would take his belt and wrap it around his hand and give us five licks a piece on our behinds. Believe me when I say we would feel those licks. We would rather mom whip us instead of Rob, even though she hit more than five times, hers weren't as hard as his.

Nico would get into trouble more often than me with Rob, which sometimes caused problems between mom and him. Mom would think he was playing favoritism because any time Nico did anything to me, he could possibly get a whipping.

Looking back at it now, I was probably being a crybaby. However, I felt like Nico always was doing something to aggravate the crap out of me.

Rob was ex-military and he liked things to be a

certain way. For some reason, Nico and I could never do it his way. He believed in a certain order and structure, which was slightly different for me and my brother. My mom had her rules of course, but his rules and regulations were a little bit different, and I think it was not necessarily because he was our stepdad, but rather because he was a man in general.

We used to think he was so mean and strict. He would tell us to do things, and we would do it, but we never seemed to do it right. It was always wrong in his eyes, so he always yelled and told us to fix stuff. I mean we couldn't even take the trash out right without something being wrong with it.

Rob did have fun with us from time to time. He and mom would play ball with us outside in the yard and do other fun things, but it was so hard to get him to smile on a regular basis. He was normally so serious and stern, so when we could say or do something to get him to smile, we felt like we had done something huge.

Growing up being raised by a stepdad was an experience that had its own unique dynamics. During my younger years, before my biological father was released from prison, Rob was the only father figure I knew. Although I understood that he wasn't my biological father and that I had another father, Rob was the one who fulfilled the role of a father in my life.

When my biological father was released from prison, around the time I was seven or eight, I had to adjust to having both a stepfather and a biological father back in my life.

This transition took some time because we did not know our biological father very well at all. Initially, we idealized him and even entertained the idea of living with him because he seemed so wonderful.

Naturally, some of it was because he didn't discipline us like our mom and stepfather did, leaving that role to them. However, I couldn't comprehend this perspective at the time and just thought he was awesome.

Whenever he picked us up and took us to his house, we loved being there. It was exciting and enjoyable. He had a good job and was dating a woman with a daughter around my age, so we had fun hanging out and going places together.

He even had a nice car. In contrast, my stepfather didn't have a nice car at the time. I vividly remember a particular incident when we were riding in my stepfather's older green car and stopped at a store.

One of my classmates happened to be there and saw us getting out of the car. They asked me, "Is that your dad's car?" Without hesitation, I replied, "That's my stepdad's car, my real dad has a nice car." and proceeded to share the details about my father's car.

I'm not sure if Rob overheard me, but later on, I reflected on my words and felt terrible for downplaying my stepdad in an attempt to make my biological father look good – perhaps even to make myself look good. As a child, I simply wanted others to see me in a positive light, but it was a thoughtless and inconsiderate thing to do.

In time, I came to understand that while my biological father may have had material possessions, my stepfather had been there consistently, taking care of us for the past seven or eight years at that time.

It was Rob who had been responsible for raising and providing for two kids that were not his own. As a child, I couldn't fully comprehend the complexities of these relationships and the responsibilities. I realize now how misguided and insensitive it was to downplay my stepdad's role in my life.

Eventually, we began to see our father's true nature without anyone explicitly telling us. My mom never spoke ill of my dad during my upbringing, particularly when I was younger.

Only when I reached a certain age, around fifteen, did she feel free to express negative sentiments about him. However, during our younger years, when we expressed a desire to stay with him, my mom never responded with statements like, "You don't know who your dad really is." or "Your dad is not a good person." or "You'll soon realize that he's not who you think he is."

Although those statements could have been easily justified and true, she refrained from making them. Instead, she would quietly retreat to her room and cry after we voiced our desire to go live with him. We only knew she had cried because Rob came and sternly talked to us, making us realize the immense hurt we had caused our mother.

Our dad started revealing his true character to us over the years all on his own. The first way he started was by him doing something that caused him to go back to prison. We never thought this would happen.

We thought he had gotten his life together and was on the straight and narrow. But unfortunately, he wasn't, and this happened around Christmas when he was supposed to buy us a boombox as a present. For those unfamiliar, a boombox was a popular portable radio and cassette player at that time.

We had been eagerly looking forward to receiving this gift for Christmas, but when he went to prison, we never received it. He tried to explain that he had left the money with his girlfriend, who was supposed to buy it for us, but it never materialized, leaving us utterly devastated.

Although some may perceive this as a trivial matter and believe we should have been more upset about our father returning to jail (which we were), for children who rarely received anything significant from their dad, this was a significant letdown.

It marked the beginning of our realization that our dad was not the person we had thought he was, and the initial excitement of having him back in our lives faded.

CHAPTER 2

Now back to the Projects. We had great times in the Projects as kids. Everyone knew everyone, and there were kids for days. We stayed outside, playing and running through everyone's yard.

Those days, parents didn't have to watch our every move. They were able to let us run around because if we did something wrong, somebody was going to tell it.

Kids weren't getting snatched up by people. Hell, if anything, people were trying to drop their kids off with somebody else. They weren't trying to take anybody else's kids.

We were at the age when we didn't know that we were poor because everyone else was poor too. We knew that having bugs and mice wasn't something rich people dealt with, but again, we were in an area where everyone was in the same boat. Mom tried to shield us from seeing as much hardship as she could. If she didn't have enough food to feed all of us, she would just feed us, and we wouldn't realize that she didn't eat.

We stayed in the "Black Folks" Projects for a couple of years then moved to the "White Folks" Projects because they were renovating the apartments. We ended up moving back there after they finished. The "White Folks" Projects were in the white neighborhood near the hospital and actually had a few white people in it.

We had an older Caucasian man as our neighbor, and he was nice to us. When we first moved in, my Grandma Almarie told him, "You better not mistreat my daughter-in-law or you'll have problems with me."

He responded, "I'll treat her just like a little white girl." My mom told me this as an adult and I thought this was hilarious. Just FYI, my grandmother didn't play. She was as sweet as she could be and would give you her last, but she would speak her mind and tell it like it I.S. is.

I don't recall exactly how long we stayed there, but I was in elementary school. These apartments looked just like the others on the other side of town.

My brother had a friend, Johnnie, who was maybe about two years older than us. One day we were playing around at the house before school and missed the bus.

Instead of going back home, the friend said we could just walk. Now the school wasn't that far, but for a kindergarten and first grader, it was far. My mom never let us walk to school, but we hoped we could walk, and she never knew.

How many of you know that didn't work at all? Remember I said we lived in an area where everyone knows everyone? I can't remember who saw us, maybe a family member or a neighbor, but as the old saying goes, whoever it was couldn't let their drawers hit the ground before they told on us.

Mom was upset because we were too young to walk down such a busy road. I promise you, that was the last time we walked to school without mom knowing. As I said before, whippings were a part of our household.

My family didn't believe in time out or just taking something from you. You would get a whipping, get grounded, and couldn't go outside. Back then, not being able to go outside was punishment for us. Now, kids don't have any problems with staying inside. They don't want to go outside and play.

My brother and I were like normal kids at that time, we stayed outside playing for the most part. Always had a group of kids to play with, no matter where we lived. Even though, as I grew older, I suffered from allergies. At some point, I was in the house sleeping most of the time because all the doctors told my mom to give me was Dimatop, which always made me drowsy. Because of this, I grew up reading books in the house.

As I mentioned earlier, we moved a lot. Looking back, some of those times were because my mom and Rob broke up. They argued a lot while we were growing up, which would cause Rob to leave and change the dynamic of the finances.

It happened often around Christmas time and the middle of the summer. Those times stick out to me because it would leave mom financially unable to buy Christmas gifts and school clothes for us or make her ask family members for help.

Now she would find a way to buy us things, it was just less than what she wanted or planned to. Mom always found a way. My mom's sisters and brothers were old enough to work at this time and would pitch in to help her buy us Christmas gifts or the clothes we needed. We were two of the oldest grandkids so they didn't have any kids to buy for yet.

Year after year this happened, and it began to start changing the way we looked at Rob. It was hurtful, not only to my mom, but to us. It left us without, a lot of times. We started wishing she wouldn't get back with him because we knew it would be the same way next time. We felt at least when it was just us, we knew what to expect, so we wouldn't get our hopes up. However, my mom took him back repeatedly over the years, and we just dealt with it.

I remember during one of their break ups, we lived with my Aunt Betty and her husband. They had an extra room and my mom, Nico and me lived in that one room for a little while. We tried not to be a bother by staying out most of the day, and going straight to our room when we got there at night. We had lived in the exact same apartment several years prior with Rob.

One night after living with them for a while, mom asked me to say a prayer that we get the new place to stay that we were waiting to hear back about. She said, "God hears kids' prayers too." So, I prayed real hard that we would get the place mom had applied for.

The next day she got a call saying that she was

approved. Mom was so happy and so were we. We were tired of not having the freedom of having our own room and just wanted our own place. I felt like God heard my prayers and I was the hero of the family.

That was my second time feeling like a hero. The first was when I was much younger, maybe two, and we lived in a hotel-type of apartment for a very short time. My brother and I were asleep, and mom was cooking something. Obviously, she was tired because she fell asleep with food cooking on the stove.

Mom told me this because I was too young to remember, but I woke up because I smelled smoke. I went into the living room where she was sleeping, shook her awake, and said, "Mama, something is on fire." Then I proceeded to go back to bed. Thank God it was not a fire, just smoke, but we could have died from the smoke if I wouldn't have woken up.

The new place that we moved to after my aunt's was a single-wide trailer in a trailer park called Mitchell Trailer Park. We liked it because Nico and I both had our own room. My mom and Rob, yes, he's back, had a room on one end with their bathroom and Nico and I were on the other side of the trailer with a bathroom between the two of us.

Overall, the moving from place to place and the arguing shaped how I wanted to live as an adult or should I say not live. I hated listening to all the arguing and never wanted to live in a drama-filled environment. We would wake up to them arguing throughout the night, or to mom packing a bag for us to leave the house, or Rob packing to leave the house.

One time we left our house to walk in the middle of the night to my grandparent's home because they got in a bad argument, and I guess we only had one car at the time. I remember this night very well because there was a snake on the side of the road, and I almost stepped on it, which fueled my mom's anger.

Thankfully they never got in a physical fight, but the arguing became a trigger for me. As soon as I heard it, I would sit and hold my breath to see how far it would go. To see if we would have to leave tonight. I never wanted to grow up and have to deal with that. I wanted to learn from my mom's situation.

I didn't want my kids to be traumatized by that type of stuff or uprooted in the middle of the night. I always dreamed of having kids in a stable home with hopefully two loving parents, but if not two, at least one that could provide for them financially with no help from anyone.

As an adult, I have a strong aversion to arguments. The sound of neighbors arguing or people fighting always invariably fills me with fear. When I got married and became a parent, I made a conscious effort to avoid disputes in front of my son. Whenever my husband and I found ourselves in a heated argument, I would quickly put a halt to the conversation, suggesting that we revisit it later.

This was especially true when my son was younger. As he grew older, I began to believe that it might be beneficial for him to witness occasional disagreements.

    I hoped that by doing so, he would come to understand that marriage isn't always a bed of roses, but with enough love and effort, couples can weather the storms together. I wanted him to understand that people could disagree but not have to leave their homes and cause undue hardship to the family because of rash decisions made in the heat of an arugment.

KIZZIE CRAWFORD

CHAPTER 3

As a child, I enjoyed going to school. On my first day of kindergarten, my mom thought I would cry when she dropped me off. Once I got into the classroom with the other kids, I sat down and started coloring like I had been there before.

I was attentive, always tried my best, and rarely got into trouble. My kindergarten teacher, Mrs. Emrich, was incredibly kind. She would call my mom to share positive things about me and write encouraging comments on my report card.

She made the introduction to elementary school enjoyable. In her class, we had the opportunity to try out for theater plays, where we would sing and dance. During these activities, I met many of the kids who would be in my classes for the next 13 years.

We would go to the playground during recess and engage in games like "Come and Get It." The boys would chase us and try to pin us up against the fence for a kiss.

How we learned to play such silly games at such a young age is still a mystery to me, but we all participated at some point. We had monkey bars, swings, and everything else to play with. School made me happy, especially since Nico was in school and couldn't play with me anymore. Recess was the absolute best part of the day.

However, there was one time when I couldn't participate in recess. It was when I had surgery. Growing up, I had an umbilical hernia, causing my navel to stick out like a Vienna sausage. It was visible even under my shirts. I don't remember it being painful, but my mom decided it needed to be addressed. So, I underwent surgery and had to stay home from school for a little while.

When I returned, I still had a bandage on my stomach and wasn't allowed to play with the other kids outside. Naturally, kids can be selfish, so they left me to sit by myself while they ran around the playground with no regard to me sitting there alone.

Years later, my son had the same condition. His navel stuck out as a baby. They said that it might correct itself but remembering what I dealt with in kindergarten, I decided to have him have this surgery as a baby so that he would not have any memory of it.

Ms. McCloud was my second-grade teacher, and this was the first time Nico and I ever had the same teacher at the same time. He ended up not getting to go to First Grade right after kindergarten.

He had to go to Junior First before he was able to start first grade, so it put us in the same grade going forward. I hated this for Nico, but we loved being in the same grade and the same class. It was almost like we were twins at that point.

Ms. McCloud was a young African American teacher who was excited about teaching, and she made it fun for us. She cared about us learning and wanted us to succeed in her class and succeed in life. She would also call mom and talk to her about things going on in class and things she thought my mom should know.

While in second grade, we would go to PE and we would play outside on the PE field as they called it. Our PE teacher, Mrs. Williams, used to tell us that the PE field was a place where we played and sat so we couldn't spit on the field. That was the rule.

I remember I had a cold one day and obviously needed to cough up some cold while we were outside. I knew the rules, so as we walked off the field, I saw a water puddle and decided that I could just spit there since it was wet anyway and not technically on the field. Mrs. Williams got in a frenzy and said I'd get a paddling for that.

Now remember, I was seven. Back then, they didn't have to ask for permission to paddle kids. This was part of the rules of the school. Once she took us back to Ms. McCloud's class, she told my teacher what happened and called me outside the room to paddle me. I had to put my hands on the wall, and she paddled me for spitting in a mud puddle.

Before I finish this story, let me tell you a little about my mom. She doesn't play about her kids. She loves us more than life itself. Mom had a quick temper, so if you get her wrong, just know she doesn't have any problem speaking her mind. She never upheld us when we were wrong but when we were wronged by anyone, she had our backs.

She always told us to never lie to her because if we made her look like a fool defending us after we had lied, it was going to be a problem. I used that same parent strategy for my kid when he was old enough to understand.

When I got home and told mom that I got paddled for spitting in a water puddle, she hit the roof. The next school day couldn't have come soon enough for my mom. She went straight to the principal's office that morning and asked to speak with Mrs. Williams.

Based on how my mom went into that office, the Principal, Mrs. Ward, thought it was best if mom didn't talk to Mrs. Williams. They would not call the teacher up there for anything. Obviously, they knew that was not going to go well. Of course, they couldn't take away the fact that she paddled me, but that was the last paddling I ever got from Mrs. Williams or any other teacher for that matter.

Obviously, Mrs. Thomas didn't get the memo on how or who my mother was because she too got a visit from mom. She was my 3rd-grade teacher. Boy, did that lady not like me. I don't know what I did to cause such disdain.

I won't be surprised if she didn't like someone in my family and just took it out on me. She was an older teacher that had been around for a long time. I felt like she used to harass me for no reason. She would always call me out about something, even if the entire class was doing it. Or just make snide remarks in response to things I said. It was crazy to me. Especially, looking back at it. I was a child, and this was a whole adult and a teacher.

One day, I finally mentioned it to Mom. Why, oh why did I do that? Mom was livid. She said she was going out there the next day. I begged her not to, but she was not hearing that. She went out to the school the next day like she promised. I guess she learned not to show her feelings to the school office because they allowed her to come to my class and speak with Mrs. Thomas directly.

I was sitting in class when Mrs. Thomas went outside the classroom to speak with mom. I don't know what was said, but when she came back, I was terrified. She didn't say anything to me at the time, but at some time throughout the day or the next day she made some off-handed comment about, "I better be careful before someone tells their mama on me." I was so embarrassed. I didn't tell mom about this statement because I didn't want it to get worse.

Thank goodness her paraprofessional loved me. Her name was Ms. Sheila. I was the teacher's pet with her. I'm not sure if it was because she just liked me so much or because she didn't like how Mrs. Thomas treated me. Not sure, but I was thankful for her. She made getting through third grade tolerable.

I used to have a speech impediment when I was a kid. Kids used to laugh at me because I couldn't say twenty, fruit, or strawberries, so I had to take speech classes. I would leave class for an hour twice a week to meet with my speech teacher. She would have many index cards with different words on it for me to say repeatedly.

I enjoyed going to this class because one, it was easy, two, it got me out of real classes, and three, it actually worked overall. I still sometimes have a hard time saying some words, but I definitely can say twenty now.

Other than Mrs. Thomas, I loved my teachers in elementary school. I was always an overachiever. I used to be the first person to raise my hand when a question was asked.

If there was any competition to be won, I would try to win. In my fourth grade class with Mrs. Harris, I won two trophies for highest grades in English and Math. I was always on the honor roll list and worked hard to get on the all A's list but was sometimes a little short of getting what I needed.

Math was my weakest subject as I got older, and reading was always my best and favorite subject. In middle school, we had this competition called Reading Books Around The World. They had different pictures of places on the cafeteria walls and as you read a certain number of books, you progressed around the room, and as you moved around the room you would get a Pizza Hut certificate for a personal pan pizza.

I was killing it. I moved around the room in no time, racking up certificates as I went. Not only did I love this because everyone could see my name on the wall, I loved Pizza Hut. You can just imagine that I was loving life.

For me, reading served as an escape from reality, offering a portal to imagine myself engaging in all the adventures depicted in those books.

If left uninterrupted, I could lose myself in reading for hours on end, whether it was sitting on the swing outside, curled up on the couch, or laying on the bed in my room.There was no shortage of reading spots; I was everywhere with a book in hand.

As I grew older, I developed a particular fondness for the Baby-Sitters Club books. I could easily envision my friends and me starting a similar club, babysitting the neighborhood kids for some extra cash. Those books were my absolute favorites.

During that time, books often included postcard-style forms for ordering more books. I would eagerly fill out these forms, providing my information and sending them back. When a box of books arrived, it felt like Christmas morning to me.

Admittedly, I never paid for the books as I was supposed to, so technically, I was stealing. However, they continued sending me books, and I kept reading and ordering them without any issues until I knew better.

While in elementary school, Nico started playing football. My Uncle Pat worked with one of the coaches of recreational football and he got Nico on the team when we were in third grade.

Now anything my brother did, if I could, I got involved in as well. So, I got on the cheerleader team for his football team. It was called the Hurricanes.

It was a predominantly all white team for both the football players and the cheerleaders. We would go to the games together, and afterwards we would all go to the local Dairy Queen for ice cream. My Uncle Pat did most of the transporting during this time. I don't recall mom being able to make it to many of the games due to work.

Unfortunately, Nico took a bad hit, and his shoulder was broken. He tried to hide it for as long as he could because he loved football, but finally mom figured out something was wrong and took him to the doctor. When she found out she made him quit, which is what he was afraid of. He never played again after that, unfortunately.

I still had a strong desire to continue cheering, even though Nico was no longer playing on the team. However, my enthusiasm was now directed toward a different team – the Packers. This team consisted entirely of black cheerleaders, and I was personally acquainted with some of the members, unlike the previous team. In truth, I had wanted to cheer for the Packers from the very beginning, but I couldn't bring myself to cheer against my brother's team. It wouldn't have felt right to be on the opposing side when it came to supporting him.

My love for cheerleading was unwavering. I absolutely loved it. We had the cutest green and white uniform, and I reveled in performing flips and stunts. Although I was sad that Nico couldn't play anymore, I was grateful that I could still cheeer.

CHAPTER 4

My mom worked hard over the years to take care of us. She was not afforded the advantages of getting child support from our father nor getting welfare assistance.

She would work numerous low paying jobs just to make sure we had what we needed. I remember going to work with her on many occasions over the years when she worked at a motel job.

She was a housekeeper at The King Frog when we were young. I know that's such a country name but it was the most popular motel in town at the time. I would help her take the sheets off the bed and remake the beds and carry dirty laundry to her cart.

When I would get tired or maybe when I went to work with her because I didn't feel well, I would lay down in the room closest to the laundry room and watch TV. Not only did my mom work there, at some point my Grandma Gloria, Grandma Almarie and my Aunt Betty and Aunt Debra worked there.

They worked in the laundry room washing and folding linen. So, it was a family affair to get to see my whole family in one place. One of them would check in on me while my mom was cleaning rooms upstairs or on the other side of the motel if I was laying down.

I was so young and didn't think twice about the fact that my mom had to take me to her job because she didn't have anyone to keep me. That was just the way it was. I used to go sit in the laundry room with whomever was working at that time and just chit chat with them. I enjoyed the smell of fresh linen coming out of the dryer.

I used to think it was so neat how my grandmothers could fold those towels and sheets so neatly. Especially the bottom sheets. Like how is that even done correctly? Well, my grandmothers were professionals at their jobs. They had it down pat.

I used to know all their coworkers/friends that worked there. Two of them that stuck out to me were a lady named Ms. Mildred and a lady named Ms. Vera. They were all like family friends because they all worked together and were going through tough times together. They would drop off or pick each other up if anyone needed them to. My Grandma Almarie was like that as well with my mom's side of the family. She would drop them off or pick them up occasionally if needed.

I grew up very close to both sides of my family. My mother's parents Gloria and Willie Owens but everyone called him Tom, had nine children with 3 of them passing away.

Two at birth and one when she was around 9 years old from sickle cell anemia. My mom was the 2nd oldest living sibling and the oldest living daughter. It was Uncle James, my mom, Aunt Betty, Uncle Pat, Aunt

Debra and Uncle Tommy. Mom helped a lot with her brothers and sisters.

Several of my uncles and aunts are close to my brother and my age so we grew up calling them by their first names, Pat, Debra and Tommy. Like I mentioned before we even lived with them from time to time due to my mom falling onto hard times.

The homes we lived in with them were always small back then with 3 bedrooms and one bath, so it was really crowded when we all lived there. However we were family and we made it work.

My Grandfather Tom died in his early 50's and my grandmother Gloria died at the age of 68. We also lost my Uncle Pat when he was in his early 30's. Pat was born with the same disease as his sister that died from sickle cell. Sickle cell is such a horrible disease and affects 1 out of every 365 African Americans.

The majority of my family has a trait of sickle cell but not the full-blown disease like my Uncle Pat and Aunt. About 1 in 13 African American babies is born with the sickle cell trait.

My grandparents were told when he was born that he wouldn't make it to be 13. God obviously had another plan because he lived long enough to get married and have two kids.

My father's parents, Almarie and Willie B, were a big part of our lives as well. My grandmother had 3 previous kids, Uncle Jerome, Aunt Daisy, Uncle Alvin, before meeting my grandfather which we called Granddaddy B.

Grandma then had two boys with him. My father being one of them and my Uncle Tony. My dad was the baby of the family and was treated as such.

Holidays were a big deal in our family. Christmas, Easter, Thanksgiving, you name it, we celebrated it. Every Easter mom would buy me a nice dress and Nico a nice suit and she would take us to Church. In our early years, we went to church on a regular basis.

As we got older, we stopped going as much until Grandma Almarie started encouraging us to go as teenagers. As a kid I loved getting dressed up for Easter to say my Easter speech.

I had long hair so mom would put pretty ponytails in my hair with bows or beads and as I got older, she would put one ponytail in the front and have the back hanging with curls in it.

I was tender headed and cried while getting my hair done so mom put a relaxer in my hair at an early age to make it easier to handle. I was thankful, but hated the fact that I didn't have fluffy ponytails like some of the other girls with natural hair.

We always had an Easter speech. We would go to my Grandma Almarie's church in Sparks, GA (which is even smaller than Adel) since we didn't have an official church home. I never wanted to miss going to church on Easter Sunday.

So much to the point that even when I was sick, I wouldn't mention it so that we could still go. I recall one time when I was about 7 or 8, I was sitting in the choir stand at church waiting on them to call us down to say our Easter speech.

Obviously, I had eaten something that made me sick, or I was coming down with something, but before I knew it, I just threw up everywhere. I was humiliated. I kept saying to my mom, "I'm so sorry, I'm so sorry", as though it was my fault.

Of course, everyone felt so bad for me and didn't blame me but I was still horrified because I was sitting in the front of the church. That was one day that I wished I didn't want to be front and center.

Christmas was my next favorite holiday. Grandma Almarie always tried to keep her family close. She was the nucleus of our family. Everyone came to her house, and not just on the holidays either, but on the holidays, she would get all her grandkids together and we would exchange gifts.

There were a lot of us, about 15. She would go out her way to get all the mothers to bring the kids over because my dad and one of my uncles weren't around to bring their kids to be part of most of the holidays. My dad and Uncle Al stayed in and out of jail and prison over the years. My other uncles, Uncle Jerome and Uncle Tony, would attend and make sure their kids were around.

We would have a great time hanging out with each other because that was about the only time we would all be together. As I stated before, Grandma was the nucleus of the family, so her sister's and brother's kids loved her and would come around on a regular basis. Even the ones that lived in other states.

Grandma was the favorite Auntie of all her neices and nephews. Cousin Deborah and her husband Richard would come visit with their 3 kids. I remember one time when they came, Cousin Deborah bought me and Nico a radio each.

I don't know how much it cost or why she bought it, but it meant so much to me. It has always stuck out in my memory but I'm sure if I would ask her about it now, she probably wouldn't remember it because it was a simple gesture to her.

It was the same with my Aunt Daisy and Uncle Larry. They were in the Air Force and were stationed all over but when they came home, I always went to grandma's house to see them or they would come see us.

Auntie would buy me earrings, or a kid's makeup kit or a beautiful necklace from another country that she visited or was stationed in. All those gifts stuck out to me. It made me feel special. Like someone saw me and thought of me even though-they-didn't-live-close.

On my dad's side, we had family reunions every year. This was a serious event in our family. It was every Labor Day weekend. If I had to guess, I would say that I attended about 90% of them over the course of my life. I always enjoyed them, and my grandmother instilled in me that family was important.

The reunions would rotate every year. It would either be in the Adel/Valdosta area, Watkinsville, GA or Pompano, Florida. Once we had it in Atlanta, GA, and I swear that was drama-filled and never happened again.

When the reunions were out of town, they rented vans so we could ride together. We even rode a school bus one time to Watkinsville. I always went with grandma because Dad wasn't around, and my mom never went to these events. She made us available to go, but she never attended.

My mother's side of the family also got together for holidays but on a smaller level. All my Grandma Gloria and Grandaddy Tom's kids and grandkids would come to her house to celebrate the holidays.

We would sometimes have a random 2nd or 3rd cousin drop by, but it was mostly the immediate family of my grandma and grandad. We would all hang out for hours, eating and talking.

On this side of the family, exchanging gifts was not a thing throughout the family but all the adults would make sure the kids had gifts even if they helped the parents buy their gifts. My mom and her siblings were close, and they all helped each other out when they needed help. The grandkids were taught the same thing. If anyone of us have any form of major hardship, we would all go together to help out if we could.

Mom raised Nico and I up to be very close as well. She told us to always take care of each other. Nico was to always look out for me since he was the oldest. He was my protector.

We grew up doing almost everything together. When you saw one, you saw the other one. My mom didn't let people come get one without the other one when we were young, and when it happened, on those rare occasions, we missed each other miserably.

I would cry and say, "Where is my Nico?", "I miss my Nico!". I was also a crybaby. I cried all the time. When my mom would leave us with babysitters or with family to go somewhere or go to work, I would cry and cry.

I remember two instances when mom left me with a babysitter, and I laid on the couch with a toy over my face crying. The babysitter was an elderly lady who kept us from time to time. She was so sick of me for crying that she called my mom to come back to get me.

Another time she left me with her sisters Aunt Betty and Aunt Debra. I remember lying in the bed with them, it was three to a bed. They tried to wake me up, and I wouldn't open my eyes.

I feel like I was doing this deliberately because my mom left me. After I wouldn't open my eyes, they tried calling my mom. When she got there, everyone was in a panic now.

At this point, I was scared to open my eyes. I knew I would get in trouble if I acted like I just wanted her to come home. So, then they took me to the hospital. This went from bad to worse. Now scared was not even the word for what I was feeling. I was terrified.

I don't even know what they eventually did to me, but I decided to open my eyes when they did it to make it look like it worked. I was such a baby. I was attached to my mom and didn't want to stay with anyone else.

I eventually got better when I was about five or

so. Maybe when I started elementary school and went to school for half a day and then went to my Grandma Gloria's house for the rest of the day.

If I had to describe myself when I was a kid, I would say I was an intelligent, kind, sweet-hearted, loving kid who loved everyone. I was loving and caring to everyone and always was willing to help anyone who needed it. I established strong bonds with all my immediate family members and didn't have favorites.

My mom always told me that I didn't see black and white, like most people. I saw purple. I was always the optimistic cheery one in the family. I rarely caused problems growing up and was always happy.

However, I must admit, I was confident and bossy from day one. My mom told me a story about how she had me all dressed up and was walking down the road when I was about 2 or 3.

She wanted to hold my hand because she didn't want me to walk out in the road. I snatched my hand from her and said in my baby voice, "No, I'm a big girl. I don't need you to hold my hand." I always thought that was funny because it, to me, was the beginning of my big personality.

I bossed Nico around all the time. When we played, I was always the one making the rules. When we had to clean up, I always delegated the duties. Nico was good at allowing me to take the lead until he hit about 16. Then it was a whole other story. OMG. He got really bossed up then. I think it was when he started smelling himself, as the old folks say.

CHAPTER 5

As I mentioned earlier, my dad was the baby of the family and was treated as such. He was the only kid that my grandparents raised who didn't work while attending school or in the summers, from what I was told.

From my understanding, he would do chores around the house to make money. Sometimes I wonder if that helped to contribute to some of his actions as an adult. Never really having any responsibility and growing up being treated as the baby.

He has an air of entitlement that I never understood. Sometimes, I wonder if that is just jail house mentality. I've read that many incarcerated men suffer from post-incarceration syndrome (PIS) which is a psychiatric disorder that affects individuals who have been incarcerated and then released back into society.

It encompasses a spectrum of psychological, emotional, and social challenges that may emerge due to incarceration. In my opinion, he has this entitled attitude to this day. Throughout his 63-year-old life, he has been in and out of prison and jail.

When he wasn't in jail or prison, most times, he was addicted to drugs which caused him to do illegal things to return back to jail. It was a vicious cycle.

As I became a teenager, and my friends started to realize how my father was, and I would wish that he had stayed in prison as opposed to being out. I know that sounds harsh but there were several reasons I felt that way.

First and foremost, he embarrassed us. I'm not even going to lie and say he didn't. When people came to us telling us, "I heard your dad was doing this..." or "I heard your dad was doing that..." It deeply affected me.

Secondly, because if he was incarcerated, he couldn't access drugs so easily. He would appear healthy and in his right mind while in prison. However, outside of prison, he appeared sickly, as is often the case with individuals battling drug addiction.

Thirdly, I felt he was safer in prison, to the extent that anyone can be safe while incarcerated. But when he was out, and engaging in illegal activities, such as theft and drugs, I was in fear that someone would hurt or even kill him. Despite not having a great relationship with my father, I never wished harm upon him and wanted him to stay away from potential dangers.

When I became an adult and he would first get out of prison, I would be able to have some type of relationship with him. During these times, he was happy to be home, hadn't started his old ways and wanted to be involved in my life.

However, it was always short lived. Once he went back to his old ways and started asking for money to support his habit, I would cut off all ties with him in an attempt to keep my peace.

This too was a vicious cycle. I have held and continue to hold resentment toward him whenever he asks me for something. My resentment stems from the belief that he was absent during our upbringing and never fulfilled his responsibilities as a parent. Consequently, I believe he has no entitlement to ask us for anything, particularly if it involves supporting his drug habit.

The most significant rift I had with my father occurred when I was around 37 years old. He was incarcerated for a minor offense and requested something from me that I wasn't willing to provide. His anger escalated to the point where he sent me a lengthy letter, approximately three to four pages long, and its content deeply hurt me.

In this letter, he uttered hurtful and untrue statements, targeting not only my mother and aunt but also my relationship with my husband, among other things. What added to the shock was the realization that my dad didn't physically write this letter. He had started losing his eyesight, making it impossible for him to write, which meant he had to verbally convey these hurtful words to a fellow inmate who transcribed them onto paper.

That was the last straw for me. Now my interactions with my father are very limited, and only happen when I see him at family functions, which are far and in between.

After this encounter, I decided to get counseling in attempt to deal with the trauma of my father's abandonment. At that time, I had started my mentoring program for middle and high school girls called Distinguished Young Ladies. I didn't feel like I could mentor them effectively if I was dealing with my own daddy issues.

I wanted to work through my issues to make sure that it not only affected me mentoring to the girls but to not cause problems with my husband. Ladies who deal with daddy issues unknowingly have issues that shows up in their romantic relationships. I wanted to make sure I dealt with my own issues and not expect my husband to compensate for what I was lacking.

I recommend anyone who has dealt with trauma or abandonment as a child to seek counseling. In the black community, counseling is frowned upon. However, if more of us dealt with our issues through counseling, we could break generational curses that a lot of black families suffer from.

I pray that eventually, my father conquers his addiction, recognizing it as an illness, and manages to put his life back on track before his time on this earth ends. This isn't just for the sake of my brother, me, or our children, but primarily for his own benefit. Witnessing him enjoy the quality of life that every individual deserves would be a heartwarming sight.

CHAPTER 6

As a kid, I was a bedwetter. I didn't wet the bed every night but on occasions I would not wake up and go to the bathroom. I would hold it as much as possible and then start dreaming that I was sitting on the toilet. OMG. That was the worst. Soon as I started peeing in the dream, I would wake up and realize that I was going in real life.

Sometimes I didn't wake myself and didn't realize it until morning or until I felt a belt or switch hitting my behind. I used to get into so much trouble for wetting the bed and it was so embarrassing.

One embarrassing time was after my dad was released from prison. On this one rare occasion, I stayed the night with my dad, his girlfriend, Ms. Phyllis and her daughter Denise. Denise was younger than me by a year. We enjoyed playing together and I had fun going over there. But on this occasion, when I stayed the night, I peed in the bed.

We were in the same bed so when I peed, she couldn't help but get wet. I woke up after I peed on myself and realized what happened. I got up quietly, grabbed a fresh pair of underwear, tip-toed to the bathroom to freshen up, returned, stuffed my wet underwear in the bottom of my suitcase, and returned to bed.

When everyone got up the next day to find out our bed was wet, I lied. I sat there with a straight face and lied. I am not proud of my actions, but I just didn't want to admit that I peed in bed when Denise was younger than me.

Of course, Denise said it wasn't her either. Ms. Phyllis said, "Denise is not known to pee in the bed." That's when I knew they knew it was me, but I still couldn't admit it. They looked in my bag to check for my wet underwear and low and behold they found my wet panties.

If I was smart, I would have kept the wet panties on and stayed in the bed since both of us were wet, but they probably still knew it was me, so whatever. I think Dad was more upset than Ms. Phyllis. She tried to be very nice about it. However, it was still embarrassing. They had to take the mattress outside and let it air dry. It was a big production. If I could have crawled into a hole and stayed there, I would have.

Another time was when my grandma got hold of me. The only whipping I ever got from my Grandma Almarie was for peeing in the bed. We had stayed the night with them, and I peed in the bed.

It wasn't any lying on this one because I was in bed by myself. She got me up that morning and got one of those skinny switches. Ya'll know what I'm talking about. Those that are easy to move back and forth. She got me by the hand and tore my little legs up.

As she whipped me, I was going round and round in circles like a top spinning on the floor. I don't know what stopped the bed wetting. Maybe I just grew out of it, I guess, because it wasn't from the whippings.

I wasn't the only bedwetter, so at least that makes me feel a little better about myself. When I was young, I always had some type of party for my birthday, so one year I wanted to have a sleepover. I cannot remember how old I was, but we were young. About five girls came to stay the night with me, and we all slept in the bed together.

When we woke up the next morning, we all were wet because someone peed in the bed. It was one of my cousins I believe, but I won't say no names. Everyone thought it was her, but she never admitted it and since we were all wet, no one could prove it. I totally knew how she felt so I tried to make light of it, but I know she was embarrassed.

Even though I grew up wetting the bed sometimes, no one knew about my bedwetting but the people in my house and family. I didn't go around smelly. It was unfortunate that some kids did, and they were bullied and humiliated by their peers. Kids are cruel and would give you a nickname that you would have for life.

It's disheartening that kids are criticized or shamed for wetting the bed when bedwetting, also known as nocturnal enuresis, is a common childhood issue. It is part of their development, and could be caused by genetic factors, hormonal issues, overactive bladder muscles, and stress or emotional triggers. The prevalence of bedwetting varies by age, decreasing as children 15-20% of preschoolers may occasionally wet the bed, while adolescence, less than 5% continue to do so.

Most children eventually outgrow bedwetting with time and appropriate support. I eventually grew out of it within that time frame without any type of treatment. I took this into consideration when my son was going through the bedwetting stage. I knew fussing and whipping him wouldn't solve the problem.

CHAPTER 7

I was a debater growing up as well. I could always debate my side of any situation. I got my way a lot because I was convincing. Especially with my Granddaddy Tom.

I could just look sad around him and he'd ask me what's wrong. I would say, "No----thing." in a sad voice. He would quickly assume something was and give me a couple of dollars and send me to the store to get some cookies or candy.

But because I was good at getting my way and debating my point, eventually, everyone started saying, "You need to be a lawyer when you grow up." I would hear this from everyone. My mom, uncles, aunts, grandfather, etc. I loved watching the Judge shows with my Grandaddy Tom.

He would sit there and watch it for hours and I would sit there with him at my grandparents' house in the room they called a den. We loved Judge Judy, The People's Court and whatever court was playing.

At some point, when people asked me what I wanted to do when I grow up, I would say, "I want to be a lawyer." I still wonder to this day, what I would have wanted to do if people wouldn't hadn't given me that idea at such a young age.

I was a people pleaser growing up. I didn't want people to be disappointed in me. I wanted to make the people who loved me proud. I grew up never wanting to cause shame or disappointment to my family. I don't know if that is always a good thing.

Yes, you want to represent your family but living a life where you are always worried about what people thought of you was not always a good feeling. It's a heavy load to carry.

When I turned 40, that feeling completely went away. I started to not care what people thought of me or how I lived my life. At the end of the day people will criticize if you are doing everything right, so you might as live your life in a way that is pleasing to God and yourself. In that order.

I like to tell young adults that the earlier you get to that point, the better your life will be. If I had gotten to that mindset at an early age, I would be ruling the world right now. Ha-ha.

Unfortunately, I never made it to law school, and it disappointed my mom a little. She always believed that I would be the first or only lawyer in the family. During regular conversations with her I would debate my point about something and she would causally respond back, "That's why you should have been a lawyer."

She didn't mean any harm when she said it, but her disappointment was evident to me every time she did. She never officially got over it until a few years ago when she realized my now profession as an Associate

Real Estate Broker makes more money than some lawyers. She's never said anything about me being a lawyer again.

No one ever had to push me growing up. Encourage and nurture, yes but push no. I was always my own worst critic. I was devastated if I got a B, let alone a C. I was so upset and wanted to do better. When we would get report cards, my mom and Rob barely looked at mine because it was always good.

Nico's was the one they wanted to see. To make sure he was passing everything and didn't have any remarks on it about him getting into trouble. That used to annoy me so much. I could come home with all A's and they were like, okay, cool, but Nico could come home with A's B's, and 2 C's, and they are super excited.

I thought I was being punked or something. I never understood it then, but now I realize different kids need different things and parents must act accordingly. Nico needed more push than me in school growing up, so mom always stayed on top of what he was doing or not doing when it came to schoolwork.

Nico and I entered middle school in 1991. We were super excited because that summer we had moved to a new home, and it was so close to school that we could walk to school. No more riding the bus.

Our home was a white house on a corner lot with a big backyard. We only had 2 bedrooms and one bath, but we still loved it. I had my own room, but Nico's stuff was in it. We had a living room and a den so Nico had a pull-out bed in the den that he slept on and put up every morning before going to school. Mom and Rob were still together at this time, and they rented this house together.

Now we were between both of my grandparents' house. We were able to walk to either of their homes when we wanted to. It would take about 10 to 15 minutes to get to either home.

Another reason why we were excited to go to school was this would be the first year that we got to change classes. We weren't in kiddie school anymore where we stayed in the same class with the same teacher all day long.

They had two teams for 6th grade. It was A team and a B team. Nico and I were on two separate teams, so we didn't have a class together. I was excited to be at the new school with the upperclassmen. However, my excitement for middle school died two weeks into school when I found myself in detention. Yes, you heard right. The Miss Goody Two Shoes was actually in trouble.

I got in a fight two weeks into my sixth-grade year. A girl in my class let another girl push her up to fight me. We were all standing outside after lunch talking when two girls came up to me.

One of the girls by the name Angela said something of the sort that she heard I was talking about her. Now if I did, I couldn't remember but it definitely wasn't anything to fight about. So, I said, "No I didn't." But her friend, the one that I feel didn't like me, went on to egg it on.

Then, of course, everyone came around to see the fight. I was never a fighter. I only fought Nico and another girl when I was at home playing, and she wanted to fight me. However, I knew I couldn't act like I was scared even though I was trembling inside.

But she made the mistake of putting her hand in my face, and I swear I saw red. I swung on her, and we both hit the ground fighting. Because this school was such a small school and Nico and I were in the same grade, he wasn't far from the scene.

He started trying to stop it, but I know he was letting me get some extra licks in while he was stopping it. I just feel that in my heart of hearts. I had the best big brother ever. This was only the first of three fights I had in middle school where my brother was around and was my protector.

When my mom was called to the school about me getting into a fight, I really wasn't worried about getting in trouble with her. I was more disappointed with myself than anything.

I never went to detention or was suspended in elementary school, but middle school started a whole new life for me. Mom always told us never to start fights but if anyone starts with us, we better hold our own.

That's why I wasn't worried about getting in trouble. She always told Nico to look out for me since I was the baby and a girl. Mom just listened to what happened and said I did what I needed to do.

I wasn't the popular girl in school, but everyone

knew me. I was the smart, pretty girl that got good grades, never got in trouble, and was the overachiever. Everyone was shocked when I got in a fight because that wasn't me.

I got along with mostly all the guys, which caused many girls to not like me if they weren't already my friend. Angela and I ended up being best friends after this fight and continued to be friends until we graduated high school.

In 7th grade, the girl that instigated the fight in sixth grade kept picking on me. She always had something smart to say to me in class. One day, I guess she decided to make her move. Since we walked home from school, we were all walking off campus at the same time. I actually think she decided to walk home that day just because she wanted to fight me. She didn't normally walk home.

Nico and I were walking home with some of our other friends, and she started talking noise and making fun of me as she walked behind me. Nico was like "This needs to stop today." I stopped halfway down the road and confronted her. I said, "What is your problem?" I don't know what happened from there, but there I go again, fighting. A water puddle was nearby, and we were on the ground, fighting and wet.

Nico watched it for a while just to make sure we got it all out of our system I guess, then he pulled us a part to stop it. He didn't get in it and as long as it was girl-on-girl, he never jumped in, he just stopped it. Thank God this fight was not on school grounds, so the principal couldn't suspend me or put me in detention even though they wanted to, because they did hear about it.

The last fight I ever got in was in eighth grade. This was the worst of them all because Nico got involved. The girl thought I liked her boyfriend. I don't know why she thought this because I talked to him in elementary school, and truly wasn't interested in talking to him like that.

She was going around school telling anyone who would listen that she was going to "beat me up" after school. Nico heard about this and said, "No one is going to touch my sister." This was the beginning of a whole lot of commotion.

She told her boyfriend, and he decided that he wanted to fight Nico. He and his friends walked up to Nico while changing classes and jumped on him. It was about 3 or 4 of them. I wasn't around and didn't see the fight. While my brother was fighting the boyfriend, the boyfriend's friends were kicking Nico while he was on the ground.

When the teachers finally came to break it up, it only showed that two people were fighting, and they were both taken to the office and suspended for a week. Nico had to go home immediately. I'm not sure who picked him up from school, but they didn't check me out. I'm assuming after they got home and heard the entire story, they realized that I was at school alone and that the girl and I were probably going to fight at some point throughout the day.

My Uncle Pat immediately came and checked me out of school. We went to my Grandma Gloria's house, and the more we told the story of how this went down, the more pissed off my uncle got. Especially because the boys jumped into the fight but didn't get into trouble.

My uncle was like my mom. He didn't play. He and his friend who was there during the time decided that it wasn't over yet. He knew that I would have to fight the girl at some point and that Nico was suspended for a week, and I'd be at school alone.

He got the genius idea that we needed to return to the school at the end of the day and wait for these kids to get out of school. He wanted Nico to fight one of the three boys one-on-one, and they were going to be there to make sure it went down just like that. But oh, it didn't stop there.

He also wanted me to fight the girl so that he knew it would be a fair fight. Of course, I did not want to fight anybody, but I knew I had to. I couldn't act scared because my uncle had just told me how it was going to go down.

We got to the school a little bit before school ended and stood on the corner by the school. Everyone at school had heard what had happened so when they saw us waiting on the corner, they knew it was going to be some mess.

They started yelling, "Ohhhh, it's about to go down." and so forth. The first boy came out and Nico went in on him. My uncle was down there with him while he was fighting, then the girl spotted me and started coming down because she figured I was there to fight her as well.

As she came up to me, she started saying, "Oh you want to fight, okay, let me take my earrings off." As soon as she went to take her earrings off, I started swinging.

She started swinging back and both of us fell to the ground. We ended up rolling in a ditch, still fighting. Nico was on one end of the street fighting in a ditch and I was further down in another ditch on the other side of the street fighting.

If you can picture this, trust and believe it was the most ridiculous thing ever in life. I didn't win this fight per se, but it taught girls to leave me alone. I didn't get into another physical fight since that day.

It isn't always about winning or losing but showing people that you aren't scared. People will pick on you if you let them, but when you stand up to them, they'll back down.

This fight cost my brother an additional week of suspension and me one week, but it was well worth it. We were still able to complete our assigned work and move to the next grade without incident. Over the next few years, we all became friends again and all was forgiven.

CHAPTER 8

In our South Georgia community, it was common for kids to start working in the tobacco fields at a young age to earn money for "school clothes." Surprisingly, all the children eagerly anticipated this opportunity because it allowed them to buy their own clothing for school.

When my brother turned 12, he began working and was able to purchase some cool clothes. So, when it was my turn, I was prepared—or so I thought. Working in the bacco field, as it was commonly known as in the South, was far from glamorous.

It involved enduring scorching heat, spending the entire day there, and returning home covered in dirt. However, I was determined. But my brother had different plans! He firmly stated that his sister would not be working in any tobacco field.

He approached our mom and promised to help buy my school clothes, and he followed through on his word. He bought my clothes, plus matching outfits: a red and blue Jordan shirt with blue shorts paired with red, white, and blue Filas. We even have a picture of us wearing those outfits together.

We didn't grow up taking trips like we saw on TV or attending summer camps. We just weren't financially able to do those things. So this trip to Jacksonville, FL would always stick out to me. Mom, Rob, Nico, and I drove down for the weekend to spend time with Rob's family.

We had a cookout and hung outside at someone's home, and we got to ride a Ferry for the first time. That was a nice experience for kids who never went anywhere. Although Rob became annoyed with us over something, it was nothing out of the ordinary as he always found something to be irritated about. Nevertheless, this annoyance did not diminish my recollection of the trip.

During my middle school years, a significant conflict was unfolding in the world. It was a period that stretched from February 15, 1989, to April 27, 1992, encompassing the Afghan Civil War, a tumultuous chapter that marked the aftermath of the Soviet Union's withdrawal from Afghanistan.

Amidst this historical time, my Aunt Daisy Marie played a remarkable role as a nurse serving in the Air Force, dedicating her time to provide medical care in the midst of the Afghan Civil War. As a middle school student at the time, I was not only learning about this global conflict in my history class but also was personally touched by it through my aunt's deployment.

It was during this period that my history teacher came up with a heartfelt idea: to write letters to the brave men and women serving far from their families during Christmas. The prospect of connecting with someone involved in the military resonated deeply with me. Instead of writing a letter to an anonymous soldier, I decided to write directly to my aunt, which filled me with a sense of pride and connection. The thought that I had an aunt on the frontlines of a war zone felt quite remarkable.

In my letter, I expressed my concern and curiosity, asking about her well-being, the conditions in Afghanistan, and whether she was experiencing fear amidst the challenges she undoubtedly faced. At that moment, my Aunt Daisy Marie was the only person I knew who was directly involved in a war, and my worries for her safety were genuine.

I wasn't entirely certain if she would have the opportunity to respond to my letter, but to my astonishment and joy, a response arrived in my mailbox the following February. This exchange of letters during such a tumultuous period of history became a significant and poignant memory in my life.

The letter stated:

Hello Kizzie:

I received your letter today and to say the least, I was overjoyed. Thank you for thinking enough about me to write. In this kind of environment, hearing from your loved one is very important.

Before I continue, how are you? Almarie told me you are doing excellent in school. I am proud of you. I know you can achieve anything you can desire. As you know with a lot of studying you can be what you want to be. There are a lot of opportunities available to intelligent young people. By the way, what would you like to be when you become an adult?

How is your family? I have not heard from Almarie but I have written her. Give her my love and tell her all is well and I miss her.

I am sure you are wondering what I am doing here in the Middle East. As you know, I am a nurse. As a result of the Gulf War, there is a need here for medical people i.e. physicians, nurses and medical technicians. am located in a safe place. Quite a distance from the actual war site.

However, our mission here is to take care of those who are injured, secondary to the war be it our people (Americans) or allies' (people who are assisting the Americans) with the war e.e Saydi's, Omanis, or the British. So far, we have not received any patients, which is a positive sign.

Despite the fact that we are bored from a lack of work, we are praying that there is no use for us here. Because just like you, we want this war to end with as little casualties as possible.

Just to give you a little information regarding my environment, I live on a base called "Tent City". It is called Tent City because all of us live in tents. I live in a tent with 2 females. All of them are nurses except one. She is a pharmacist.

We all sleep on cots with sleeping bags. We are fortunate though because our tent is air conditioned, and we have electrical lights. This is done by way of a generator. In addition, to living in a tent we have a tent that is a *latrine (toilet) and we have a tent that has shower stalls.*

This is probably hard for you to imagine. But, if you have seen the show "Mash" then you can picture it; because; we live in an environment similar to "Mash" just a tiny but more sophisticated. (smile)

My experience here has been quite interesting. If I did not have a husband, I would be grateful for this opportunity. But I do miss my family.

Which brings me back to you. Having kind people like you make being far away from home a little easier to bear. So, I'll say thank you once more. You continue being smart and remember you are a very special person. Don't strive to be like me but be the best you can be which I'm confident will make us all proud.

Love you
Aunt Daisy

This letter held immense significance in my life. I've cherished it over the years, preserving it in a shoebox alongside correspondence from friends and letters from my father during his time in prison. Among all these letters, none can rival the place of importance that this one holds.

I found great joy in knowing that my words could bring a glimmer of happiness to my aunt's day. It was meaningful to her that I invested the time and effort to craft a heartfelt message. In return, her response to me was equally poignant and touching, mirroring the depth of emotion that my initial letter had conveyed to her.

During this war, Afghanistan experienced a significant level of violence and upheaval, with numerous battles, displacement of civilians, and human suffering.

Tens of thousands of Afghan civilians and combatants lost their lives, and many more were injured or displaced. The exact number of casualties can vary widely, with some estimates suggesting that hundreds of thousands of people may have died during the Afghan Civil War and its aftermath.

It's truly remarkable to think that my aunt was a participant in such a pivotal period in this nation's history, marked by the loss of countless lives, yet she was fortune to return home to us safe and sound.

CHAPTER 9

In my final year of middle school, I decided to get in band. I attempted to get in while in 6th grade but they didn't let me play the instrument that I wanted to play.

They wanted me to play the clarinet and that was not what I wanted to do. So, after a month or two, I quit. All the girls played the clarinet, or the flute and I didn't want to be like everyone else. I wanted to stand out. I wanted to play the saxophone.

There weren't many girls at that time playing the saxophone. So, in 8th grade I joined again and this time my band director allowed me to play what I wanted to play which was the tenor saxophone.

This worked out better because the school had saxophones that we as students could borrow and not pay for. They didn't have clarinets that we could borrow. Mom would have to pay a monthly fee to rent one or must buy one.

In 6th grade, she rented one for me and had to pay about $35 a month, and I didn't want her to have to do that. Once I quit, she was able to take it back and not have that bill. While in the band, we played at football games and got to go to band competitions in other states. My first time going to Atlanta was with the band.

I remember walking into the hotel we were staying at and seeing the wrestler Junk Yard Dog, Luke, and the 2 Live Crew. That was the first time I ever saw a famous person. We were all so excited. Luke and the 2 Live Crew was nice enough to take a picture with all the kids that wanted a picture. We all squeezed in, almost ripping the girls' fishnet stocking, while our band director took the picture.

Band was my first taste of traveling outside of family reunions. I'm thankful that mom allowed me to be in the band and attend most of the events. She always tried to make it where I could have money to buy food at the concession stands on our break at the games or travel to the competitions.

It was such an exhilarating feeling to be able to go to different places and meet new people. It definitely was a no-brainer for me to join the band in high school.

Deborah Bradley was my band director in high school. She was no-nonsense. She always expected excellence from us. When I first started in 9th grade, I was the third chair saxophone. My good friend Amy was 2nd chair. Now you would think that being third chair is pretty good but truthfully, it was only 3 of us playing the tenor sax and that was last position.

I ended up getting second chair in 11th grade but that too was because the first chair graduated the year before. Now don't get me wrong, I could play, I just was not the best player. I never learned the fight song. Don't tell Ms. Bradley, she never knew.

That song always was so loud and fast that they couldn't tell who was playing and who wasn't. I never learned it because it was so fast that I could never get the rhythm down. Rhythm and coordination were always a struggle for me.

That's why I never made the cheerleading squad since elementary school or never made the drill team. I tried out for both in high school but never had the routine down enough to make the team or squad.

Band was my thing, even though I hated the uniforms with a passion. It was black pants with gold and white stripes down the sides, a black, white and gold jacket and a big bucket-like hat to match.

The hat had a strap to go under your neck to keep it on. Whenever we took a break after our half time show, we had to take our hats off. All the girls' hair would be matted to their head because of the sweat and the bucket-like hats.

It was horrible. All the girls hated having to walk around like that. All the cheerleaders and drill team members didn't have that problem i.e. that's why I wanted to be one of those. They had cute outfits and cute little heels and no hats. I wanted to be on the drill team so bad, but it just wasn't meant for me.

As band members, we became a family no matter your race or age. Everyone who joined the marching band was in the same band class, went to the games on the same bus, and attended the same concerts and competitions for years.

This was the only time we made real friends with

upper and underclassmen. I remember going on a trip to Destin or Panama City for a band competition, and we all stayed at a hotel.

It was 4 of us to a room. A lot of the girls were going to get in the pool and asked me if I was going to get in. I was like, I don't have a swimsuit. My friend Amy came to the rescue. She had two and said that I could use hers. I don't know if I just didn't bring one because I didn't think we were going to get in the pool or was it because I didn't have one.

Pools weren't something we did growing up. Mom couldn't swim and we were never taught to swim. We had one of the kiddie pools when we were growing up but you couldn't swim in those or drown. Where I was from, majority of the black kids didn't know how to swim.

As an adult, I was determined that my son was going to learn how to swim. I put him in class after class until he could swim like a fish. By the 3rd time, he was about seven, he said to me, "Mom, I know how to swim, don't you have anything else to do with your money?" I thought it was hilarious.

My response was, "Don't worry about what I do with my money. My goal is to make sure you can swim anywhere in case you are out with friends, and they throw you in a pool or ocean." He learned to swim very well after that summer and I found something else to do with my money.

Actually, that is why I didn't have a swimsuit even though we were going to the beach and a pool. My mom didn't want me to get in because I didn't know how to swim. As a mother now, I can totally understand that. At the time, I was not happy about it. Even though Amy offered to give me the swimsuit, I only wore it around the pool. I didn't get in because I knew my mom would be upset if she found out or if something had happened to me.

On all the trips that we took such as to Destin, Panama City, Troy, Alabama, Atlanta, Myrtle Beach and so forth, I got the name "Hollywood" by Ms. Bradley. I always had on shades trying to look cool and no matter where we went, my girlfriends and I always attracted the boys. Every out-of-town game and every out-of-town competition we got someone following behind us to the bus or to the competition area, trying to holler at us.

Keisha and Chasity were my road dogs during the band trips. We were in the same class and had known each other since elementary school. Remember, it was only one of each school. We always sat together, stayed in the same rooms, and hung out on our breaks at the football games. We fell out on a regular basis but always made up.

Shayla came to high school my last year in high school and joined the band. I enjoyed having her with us. She was always the life of the party. She and I are the only ones who still talk on a regular basis as adults.

Social media and class reunions is how most of us stay in contact with what each other is doing. Most of us went our separate ways after high school.

CHAPTER 10

Before starting high school, we all had to figure out what path we wanted to take in high school. We had the general (for anyone not going to further education), vocational prep (for technical school) and college prep (for anyone going to college).

It was not a question on what path I was going to take because I knew college was what I was going to do. This meant the course would be more tailored to get us ready for college, and you had to take certain classes that would guarantee that you would have all the prerequisites you need for college such as Pre-Algebra, Geometry, Algebra, 2 foreign languages and so forth.

Math was always the worst for me. I tried so hard and studied more in those classes than any of them. My worst math class was Geometry. I couldn't understand the concept to save my life. My first teacher was Mrs. Bachelor, and I barely passed the class with a C.

She couldn't explain the concept enough to me for me to pass not one test. I went home crying many days, frustrated and upset because I just couldn't figure it out. After the first semester, I asked to be changed to another teacher. I was put in Ms. Mitchell's class. Unfortunately, I still never learned geometry, but I did pass the class with a B.

Ms. Mitchell tended to give the same work

repeatedly, so if you failed it the first time, she would give us the answers in class and a few days later, she would forget and give us the same work again. Didn't hurt my feelings at all. Now if someone put a gun to my head and asked me what the geometric sequence or any other question related to geometry, I would be dead as a doorknob.

Literature was always the best class for me because I loved to read and could read well. I always raised my hand to read when we had to read a novel out loud or if the teacher asked the answer to a particular question.

I never sat in the back, always in the front or middle. I used to have to sit in the front because I couldn't see the chalkboard, but in 8th grade, I got glasses.

From 8th grade forward, I wore glasses. I was only supposed to wear them during school but because I thought they were cute, I started wearing them all the time, which in turn made me dependent on them.

I had the red Sally Raphael glasses, and I thought I was fly. Now I look back at my pictures and ask myself, "Why didn't anyone tell me I looked a hot fool." For the young people reading this who don't know who she is, go look her up.

While getting adjusted to high school, my home life took a turn for the worse. Mom and Rob separated for the last and final time. This was not on good turns to say the least. The details are a little foggy, but I remember the aftermath.

We left the house to go stay with Grandma Gloria and left everything there, including our clothes. That year Rob help to purchase my school clothes like he always did when they were together. However, for some reason, he ripped up my clothes while we were gone.

Literally slashed them with a knife. I realized this when we were allowed back into the house to get our clothes. When we got back to our grandmother's home and started to unpack I saw that mine was ripped, completely through and through.

It was no salvaging them. We looked at my mom's and brother's clothes and found that only mine had been cut. I was baffled. Totally didn't understand the logic. He and my mom had the falling out, why didn't he cut her clothes instead of mine?

The only thing I could think of was that since he bought them, he knew it would hurt my mom financially to buy me all new clothes. He just didn't realize that it hurt me more because I was just a kid. There were also clothes that I loved, and some were irreplaceable to me.

That bothered me for a long time. Of course, they were replaced in no time with the help of my mom and family, just not the exact clothes. Before we got to this point, Rob, Nico and I had started having run ins more and more as we got older.

He would call mom at work to tell her something that we did and then she would feel that she had to be the mediator between us and didn't always know who to believe.

He dealt with us more because he was home in the evening with us while my mom worked evening shifts at a truck stop in Sparks. On a normal afternoon, I would come home from school and cook dinner for the family.

I cooked full meals at the age of 13. Fried chicken, rice, gravy and green beans was the type of meal that we would eat. I cooked often because my mom worked in the evenings.

Nico eventually started cooking sometimes at some point as well. Rob still worked at Del-Cook and would get home about 5 or 6 every day. My mom didn't get off until 11:00 at night. Therefore, we were home with Rob after school until we went to bed.

Rob saw things that were happening more than my mom did sometimes. For instance, he would ease drop when were on the house phone because of course, at that time, cell phones were non-existent.

He would tell mom things that he heard or thought he heard and of course we would deny them. As you can imagine this type of stuff caused tension in the home.

He once told my mom that on my way to my grandmother's house, he followed me and saw that I was meeting up with boys. Now that was so not true! When my mom asked me about it, I just couldn't believe he told this on me.

I kept racking my brain, trying to remember if anyone stopped me or came up to me while I was walking to account for his statement, but I truly couldn't. When he got mad at me or my mom, he would suggest that I was fast and was going to end up pregnant.

So, you can imagine how hard it was for mom to know who to believe. I don't know what the final straw was for them, but we didn't help, and I'll be forever sorry for our part in this.

Stepdad and step-kid's relationships can be very tricky. As a step-kid, we think it's all because they aren't our real dads, but in actuality, it's just a dad, kid relationship that can be challenging.

But we don't know the difference because our real dad wasn't in the picture. I had friends who had stepdads and they all complained about them as kids. So, I know it wasn't just Rob and it wasn't just us, it was a combination of us and the situation.

Soon after the split, Rob left home and went back to his hometown. They were buying the home as an owner financing loan so they didn't have to sell the home due to the break up.

However, mom was not able to pay the mortgage alone, so she decided to rent it out while we go stay with our grandma. By this time, my grandfather Tom had passed.

Grandma was there along with my uncles Pat and Tommy. This was not a comfortable situation, but we did what we had to do, and we were thankful to have somewhere to go.

My mom was now working at night at Adel Truck

Stop so she would sleep in the day in my grandmother's room. It was my job to wake her up to go to work at night and then I would sleep with my grandmother at night while my mom was working.

Nico slept on the couch or in the room with my uncles. After about a year of this, my brother and I were so over it! We approached our mother with a heartfelt request to return home and regain our own space. However, we understood that the only way to make this a reality was to offer financial assistance to our mother.

Our journey toward financial independence had already begun with summer employment. At the ages of 14 and 15, Nico and I had worked alongside our mom at a truck stop in Sparks, where I served as a waitress, and Nico took on the role of a janitor while our mother worked as the cook.

Now, at the ages of 15 and 16, we were eager to transition into year-round employment. Without hesitation, we made the decision. I started working as a waitress at Adel Truck Stop, where my mother now worked, and maintained this job throughout my high school years. Meanwhile, Nico secured a position at Western Sizzlin, a local steakhouse in Adel. Every payday, we contributed a portion of our earnings to assist our mother in covering the household bills, and this arrangement proceeded without any issues.

In addition to our financial support, our Granddaddy B played a crucial role by co-signing a loan for our mother to cover utility expenses. This was to ensure that we had the necessary resources to go back to living on our own. My Grandma Almarie generously offered to contribute $250.00 each month toward our mortgage payments until mom was able to get situated.

Their unwavering support reflected their understanding of our mother's tireless efforts and the profound significance of reclaiming our family home. They both was resolute in their determination to prevent our mother from losing her home and to grant us the freedom to once again reside in the place we cherished as our own.

Not only did I love being home, I loved having my own money. I was able to get my hair done bi-weekly, buy clothes I needed, and pay for trips that I went to for band or school. It was the simple things for me.

I had friends who didn't work and couldn't do these things. I didn't envy them at all. Once I became independent, mom didn't have to give me money or buy me anything else while I was in school or college.

I never let the job interfere with school. The Manager, who was named Robin, worked around my school schedule. I would get out of school around 2:00, ride the bus home, get dressed and walk to work. The job wasn't far from home, but I had to walk over a bridge to get there. When I had band practice, I would get rides from other parents to drop me off at work directly from band practice.

When I turned 16, my grandmother Almarie took me to Adel Banking and co-signed for me to borrow

$300. I will never forget this. She did this as a way for me to gain credit. She did this for almost all of her grandkids and she had a lot of them, about 15. I got a checking account and started learning how to balance a checkbook.

Grandma was passionate about teaching any of her grandkids that would listen to her the importance of good credit and paying your bills. I paid the $300 back to the bank with no problems. This was the beginning of me building credit and being able to borrow money from an actual bank.

Most adults that I knew at that time were not able to go to an actual bank. They would go to other types of financial institutions because they didn't have to have great credit. Which in turn, caused them to pay higher interest rates on loans.

I give my grandmother full credit for teaching me this valuable lesson at 16. Though I, too, eventually went to finance companies to borrow money when I got older, but I knew the difference and didn't make it a lifetime situation. It was only for a season. Most of my friends didn't have someone who was able to take them to the bank or teach them the importance of good credit.

When my son turned 16, I took him to the bank to open a bank account and I added him to one of my credit cards to help him build credit. His credit at the age of 19 is just as good as mine because of it.

Also at 16, I got my license. I was adamant that I was going to start driving and gaining my independence as soon as I could. I must credit my learning to drive to Rob.

He started teaching me when I was 12 and 13. He would take me driving down the dirt road that was near our trailer on a regular basis. For that I will be truthfully appreciative.

Nico also would let me drive when I turned 15 and he had a car. When I went to get my license on my birthday, I got them on the first attempt. Overall, I was good at driving but like most all teenage drivers, I got into a couple mishaps. One in particular was when my grandfather, allowed me to drive his truck.

First things first, Granddady B never let anyone drive his truck. But for some reason he allowed little ole me to drive it while he was out of town. I went to the laundromat in the truck, and I parked it and jumped out the car. In actuality, I inadvertently put the car in reverse before exiting out the truck.

I sprinted back into the truck to catch it before it caused any damage. Thankfully, I was able to gain control of the truck before it hit something and repositioned it back into park.

Or so I thought. Obviously, the gears had issues, or I had issues but unfortunately for me, I put it in reverse AGAIN. This time, I was not able to enter the car in time to prevent it from hitting the car parked in the other parking space behind it.

I was in utter shock. I called my mom, who was home and only five minutes away. I was crying so hard, she could barely understand me, but she came immediately to my aid.

The police were called by the owner of the vehicle and again I was crying so hard, the police officer didn't even give me a ticket. He felt so bad for me that he only gave me a warning.

The car I hit belonged to the lady who worked at the laundromat. So, I begged her not to call her insurance company. I told her that I would pay for the damages out of pocket to prevent the insurance claim going on my grandfather's insurance.

The car only had a scratch on it from the truck scrapping it as it hit it on the side. The car belonged to her father, so she had to ask for his approval. He agreed and I was so forever thankful. Now this was only part of this story. I still had to tell my grandfather that I had wrecked his beloved truck that he didn't allow anyone to drive.

Thank goodness, it was only a broken headline on the back of his truck that I was prepared to pay for. When my grandparents got home, I went over to take the truck back and tell him about the mishap. I was so nervous.

As I was telling him about what happened, my grandmother was smirking. I didn't understand why. However, she thought it was funny because she always thought my grandfather loved this truck entirely too much. Surprise surprise, my grandfather took the news better than I ever thought he would.

He even paid to fix his own busted light even though I offered to take care of it. My cousins always laugh at this story because they swear, I was the favorite grandchild because no one else would have been able to get away with that so freely.

Not only did I not have to pay to get my grandfather's truck fixed, as luck had it, the girl's father turned out to be someone I knew. He came into the truck stop where I worked on a regular basis, and he had a body shop.

When he realized it was me, he told me not to worry about it and that he had lent that car to his daughter, and she was supposed to have brought it back to him a long time ago. Therefore, he wasn't worried about her riding around with the scratch on the car. Luck was definitely on my side.

CHAPTER 11

This is probably a little too personal, but I want to write it to show the type of relationship mom and I had.

At 16, for some odd reason I just assumed that girls find their first loves and then become intimate with them. Now I know how crazy that sounds, but then, that's what I thought and saw in my community.

Some of this concept more than likely came from my mom and dad dating at that young age, even though I knew that wasn't a good example to go by. Growing up, mom and Rob were always were very open to discussing sex with us, as early as we were old enough to ask questions.

They never shied away from the subject and never shut us down when we asked questions. My mom was determined that I wasn't going to get pregnant as a teenager and make the same mistakes she made and a lot of young girls in our town.

Girls were getting pregnant as young as 13 and having multiple babies prior to graduating during the time that I was in middle school and high school. It was a vicious cycle in our community where girls were following in the footsteps of their mothers or the people around them.

Mom always said, "You should wait until you get married, but if you just think you are so in love and think you just got to do it, come to me and I'll take you to get birth control."

When she said this, she really meant it. When I was 13, I went to an OBGYN for the first time and the doctor recommended that I get on birth control pills to help regulate my period and stop the horrible cramps that I suffered. But I said no. I remember that day like it was yesterday. They didn't understand why I wouldn't do it since it would lessen the pain during my menstrual time.

My reasoning was, I wasn't ready to have sex and mom always told me to come to her before I had sex. I didn't want to be in the heat of the moment and not think twice about it because I was already on the pill. I wanted to have a conversation with my mom like she said I could.

So after dating my first serious boyfriend for about six months, I thought I was so in love with him that we could take the next step, so mom would have to live up to her word. One day I went to her and said, "Mom, I've been dating my boyfriend for 6 months and I think I might want to have sex with him eventually.

I truly have to give it to my mom; she kept it very cool. I wouldn't have ever thought she was screaming in her head, "What the hell are you talking about?" But all she said was "Are you sure?" I said yes and she said okay. She said she would schedule me an appointment to go to the doctor.

Now obviously, she went to my brother and said, "You need to talk to your crazy ass sister because she wants to have sex with this boy.", because one night, when Nico came to walk with me from work, he asked me about it.

I knew then that mom had asked him to speak with me about it. Not sure how the entire conversation went, but it was supposed to be his job to convince me not to have sex. After a couple days, it was a moot point because my then boyfriend broke up with me because he wasn't a fan of virgins. Who would have known that.

I knew many girls at school had probably already had sex by then but still. Was that so common that guys expected 16-year girls to be experienced?

Anyhow, it was a blessing in disguise. I was not mature enough to deal with such intimacy at that time. Kids don't realize that sex is more than a physical act, especially for girls. Girls get emotionally involved after sex and think the relationship will last forever, while some guys look at it like it wasn't anything other than a physical act and they are on to the next.

So many girls had gotten reputations at my school for sleeping with different guys and the guys go back and tell everyone for bragging rights. I never ever wanted to be one of those girls. Needless to say, I didn't get on the birth control pill at this time. This meant I would have to have this conversation again in my lifetime.

One day, at my workplace, in the aftermath of

my breakup, I found myself engaged in a conversation with a familiar face who was named Chris. Chris was a co-worker of mine at the Truck Stop, a fellow student from my school, and remarkably, an ex-boyfriend from my 8th-grade year. Back then, our young romance had come to an end as I transitioned to high school, given the fact that he was one year behind.

As I poured my heart out to Chris about my recent breakup, I was met with genuine sympathy and a willingness to lend an ear. It had always been evident that Chris held a lingering affection for me since our middle school days, yet he had never crossed any boundaries or uttered any disrespectful words during my previous relationships.

He had consistently been a supportive and approachable friend, even when I was dating others. However, with my newfound single status, Chris decided to take a chance, to "shoot his shot," as they say. From that point forward, Chris became a permanent and inseparable presence in my life. We were practically joined at the hip; if you saw one of us, you were certain to find the other close by.

Both our families embraced our relationship, fostering a warm and loving connection between them. Chris, with his sweet and kind-hearted nature, held me in the highest regard, always willing to go the extra mile for me.

Similarly, I fell hard for him and reciprocated his care by engaging in romantic gestures and imparting financial wisdom gleaned from my grandmother.

In essence, we complemented each other beautifully, though there were some distinctions. While I possessed an outgoing and fast-paced disposition, Chris tended to be more reserved. These differences would present its challenges down the road, but at this stage, we were deeply in love, willing to look past our differences.

Our bond was so strong that it extended beyond the workplace and school. We often visited each other in our spare time, making sure to bridge the gap between our homes. Chris's sister's residence, where he lived, was conveniently close to my house, facilitating frequent hand-in-hand strolls through Adel, which became a common sight for our neighbors.

Our connection remained steadfast through high school milestones, as we attended prom together during my junior and senior years, and again during his senior year. Eventually, Chris acquired a car, which was a little red Nissan. We were so happy about his new car and I found myself behind the wheel almost as often as he did.

He allowed me to drive, to ensure that I had reliable transportation, a testament to his dedication. Even though I tried to dissuade him, he insisted on showering me with lavish gifts for my birthday and Christmas, a tangible expression of his commitment to my well-being.

Chris readily joined my family on reunions, specifically those on my dad's side, indicating the depth of affection my family held for him. Their admiration for Chris was well-founded; he truly was an outstanding guy. My brother and Chris formed a strong bond and often spent time together. Nico, who was always protective of me when it came to the guys I associated with, felt genuinely at ease around Chris.

Unlike some of the more slick guys pursuing my attention, Chris came across as sincere and straightforward, which earned him my brother's trust. We frequently went on double dates, often accompanied by my brother and his girlfriend.

During our high school relationship we rarly argued unlike many of the other couples our age. Chris, in particular, was not one to engage in conflicts; his easygoing nature was a defining trait. Whenever I found myself upset about something, he would simply listen attentively, allowing me to vent until the storm of emotions subsided. What stood out was that he never engaged in arguments or pushed back, which often made me feel guilty for being upset in the first place.

In my senior year, Chris' junior year, the recruiters for the military came to our school to have us take the ASVAB test. Back then, everyone needed to take it. I had no idea what this test was all about, but it would decide if you could go to the military or not. The military was something I never thought about at all.

I always planned to go to college to get my law degree. However, for some reason, I did decent on the test, meaning recruiters started calling me. A Navy recruiter reached out and started discussing all my options and how I could go to school in the military and not have to pay student loans.

This piqued my interest. I knew that when I went to college, if I didn't get a full ride, which I figured I would not, I would have to take out loans to get through college. Then I started hearing other kids in my class who decided to go to the military. It became a whole thing for the class of 1996.

After speaking with my family, I decided I was going to join the Navy. I would have loved to join the Air Force like my Aunt Daisy and Uncle Larry but my score wasn't high enough. So, the Navy it was.

The more I delved into understanding the military and where I would be stationed, which happened to be in San Diego, California, the greater our concerns grew about maintaining our relationship. Given that Chris had not yet reached his senior year in high school, pursuing a military career alongside me wasn't a viable option at that time.

We deliberated long and hard about our future together, and ultimately arrived at the decision to marry right after high school, with the intention of him accompanying me when I got stationed.

Interestingly, prior to making this decision, I had been among those individuals who expressed reservations about high school engagements and marriages. I held the belief that such unions might result in people feeling tied down too hastily. Yet, here I was, becoming the person I had once questioned, getting engaged during high school and planning to wed immediately after graduation.

It's worth noting that, despite our commitment to each other, Chris and I had not yet engaged in an intimate relationship. Following the previous experience with my first real boyfriend, I was determined to take things at a slower pace, a choice that Chris fully respected and supported.

So about ten months of dating Chris bought a beautiful ring and proposed in front of my mom and grandmother in the living room of my house. Everyone seemed to be happy and accepted my decision. At least almost everyone. My Aunt Daisy and Uncle Larry, who have now retired from the military and were now living in Valdosta, knew I was crazy and my Auntie voiced her opinion along the way.

However, it didn't change our minds. The plan was set. We were officially engaged, we were going to get married after graduation, and I was going to boot camp. Once it was over, Chris would fly to San Diego, where I would be stationed to start my training classes.

He would finish high school, yes, that's what I said, in San Diego, and then, we'll figure out the rest. You remember at the beginning of this book, that I said this only lasted a few months? Well this is where it started unraveling.

I went through the process of obtaining all my Navy gear and attended one of the swearing-in ceremonies at the Navy office in Valdosta. Another swearing-in ceremony was scheduled in Jacksonville, Florida, before I would officially become part of the

United States Navy as an E2.

However, as the date drew nearer, I found myself having second thoughts. It became clear to me that this was not the path I wanted to pursue. My true desire was to attend Valdosta State University and deal with potential student loans later on if I had to. My recruiter was furious with my decision. He attempted to pressure me into going in as planned, emphasizing that there was no turning back once I had already taken the oath.

However, my mother, being the supportive and protective figure she is, was not about to let this situation proceed as it was. She firmly informed the recruiter that if I no longer wished to pursue a Navy career, he couldn't force me to do so.

He resorted to trying to guilt-trip me, insinuating that my decisions were influenced by my boyfriend, suggesting that I didn't want to leave him. While there might have been some truth to that, ultimately, my choice boiled down to my own desires—I simply did not want to join the Navy.

Later, I observed many of my friends who had enlisted and found themselves unhappy, returning home shortly after their departure. While some individuals did make successful careers in the Navy, the majority of my peers from high school, particularly the girls, did not.

With my acceptance to Valdosta State University, Chris and I decided to postpone our marriage plans. We remained engaged and opted to tie the knot a couple of years down the road when the timing felt right.

CHAPTER 12

Prior to our graduation, our school held an awards day ceremony, a formal event requiring us to dress up. On that day, I was fortunate to receive a small book scholarship, which would prove immensely helpful during my first year at VSU.

After the event, I had an errand to run, involving paying a bill for my mother at First Franklin, a loan company conveniently located on my way home. Upon entering the office to settle the bill, the Manager, Lynn, unexpectedly inquired if I was seeking employment. At the time, I hadn't been actively job hunting, but the opportunity piqued my interest. Given the choice, I preferred working at First Franklin over my current positions at the Truck Stop and Western Sizzlin.

During my senior year, I had managed to secure an arrangement that allowed me to leave school early and head straight to work. Adel Truck Stop had recently reduced my hours, so I had taken a job at Western Sizzlin with the intention of eventually quitting the Truck Stop.

However, they asked me to stay on for a few days each week, so I found myself juggling both jobs simultaneously. I inquired about the job's requirements and responsibilities, and Lynn informed me that I'd need to undergo a typing test to assess my words-per-minute typing speed.

This didn't faze me, as I had recently taken a typing class at school and my typing skills were in excellent shape. I went and expressed my gratitude to my teacher for imparting this valuable skill, as it played a crucial role in my job application success.

I accepted the job offer and planned to start working after our graduation but before commencing college. As a result of my new job, I made the decision to quit my position at the Truck Stop while retaining my weekend shifts at Western Sizzlin.

The reasons behind my choice to maintain two jobs at such a young age remain a bit of a mystery. Maybe because I found fulfillment in earning my own income and contributing to my family's financial stability, ensuring our bills were consistently paid.

In the summer of 1996, my nephew was born. Vanico Dreshawn Thomas. He was the cutest baby boy I had ever seen. Everyone fell in love with this little boy. He was mom's first grandchild, and my first and only nephew to this day. I took him around like he was my baby. He was good practice. He went to church with me and Chris, I would take him to my friends' house and just paraded him around Adel.

People would ask me if he was ours, and I would quickly say "No ma'am." or "No sir, he is my nephew." By the time I was in my first year of college good, he was staying with us. At this point, it felt like my mom had another child and I had a little brother.

I didn't have a car when I first started college

and because I couldn't afford to stay on campus, I commuted back and forth from my mom's house to Valdosta which was about 30 minutes.

I would either drive my mom's car or my brother's car. Which meant that I would have to drop them off to work prior to going to school. So sometimes my day would consist of getting up at 5:30 a.m. to get ready, drive Nico to Tifton where he worked at Shaw which was 30 minutes away. The opposite of Valdosta.

I would drop him off by 7:00, drop my nephew off at 7:20 at the daycare in Sparks, halfway between Tifton and Adel, and then drive to Valdosta to make an 8:15 class.

Or on the days Nico was off, he would take me to school and pick me up. He was never on time. It would drive me crazy. I would call him to ask where he was, and he would say I'm almost there, knowing he is 20 minutes away.

When I had to take mom to work, it was a little bit easier. She worked at the school in Adel, so I would just have to take her to work and then go to Sparks to drop off Dre. I was responsible for dropping off Dre on the days Nico had to work because Dre couldn't get dropped off before 7:00, which was exactly when Nico had to be at work in another town. This is something I had to do until I was able to buy my own car.

My first college refund check came, and I went to buy my very own first car. Nico got off lucky because mom had given him her old car, but I had to buy my own. But that's okay, because she signed with me to get it and I payed the downpayment that was needed. It was a red Pontiac Sunbird. It was not new, but I loved it because it was mine and it was red. I felt accomplished being able to buy my first car.

CHAPTER 13

I didn't have the typical college experience, and to this day, I regret it. I vowed that my children wouldn't have to go through the same.

Financially, I couldn't secure enough aid to cover all my expenses. My Aunt Daisy, however, was a strong advocate for me to stay on campus and tried to assist me in getting financial aid.

I applied for student loans in addition to the Hope Grant and Pell Grant I received. Unfortunately, even with these resources, it still fell short of covering the costs of room, board, and my meal plan. Initially, I wasn't too disheartened by this because I knew that if I stayed at home and saved money instead of living on campus, I could still manage to work.

Staying on campus would have meant having no extra funds for purchasing a car, and the on-campus jobs didn't pay much. Given that I was accustomed to earning a decent income and contributing to my family's finances, I recognized that this would significantly alter both my personal and household financial dynamics.

Living at home and commuting to school meant I missed out on the typical college experience that everyone else seemed to enjoy. I didn't forge as many friendships and didn't attend the school's events like games and step shows.

Instead, I found myself either juggling two jobs or working an extended 40 to 48-hour workweek. During my first year of college, I joined the team at First Franklin but eventually decided to leave my job at Western Sizzlin after a few months.

At the loan company, I worked for 25 hours a week, attending classes until noon and then working from 1:00 p.m. to 5:00 p.m. I found satisfaction in working in an office, dressing professionally, and interacting with members of the community who visited.

Working in such an environment held a certain prestige, especially considering that few black individuals were employed in similar offices at the time. In fact, I was not only the only black person but also the youngest in the office. Adel was a town where I didn't see to many people that looked like me in high or professional places.

Though this job held prestige, unfortunately, the compensation was meager, at just $5.00 an hour. To put it in perspective, that amounted to only $125.00 a week. While it's important to consider the different economic landscape of that time, $5.00 an hour still wasn't a favorable wage.

Ironically, I ended up spending more on clothes to maintain a professional appearance at work than I was actually earning. To afford these clothes, I resorted to obtaining various credit cards during my college years.

It seemed that once you entered college, credit

card companies believed you could easily manage credit cards. I consistently made timely payments, but I did accumulate substantial debt while purchasing work-appropriate clothing. My job primarily involved making phone calls to individuals who were behind on their bills and processing new loan applications for those who visited in person.

As I mentioned earlier, I strongly suspect that I was hired partly due to my ethnicity, as it likely fulfilled a diversity quota. Moreover, they might have thought it would be more effective to have someone from the same racial background communicate with their black customers, in an attempt to get a response. I understand this might sound unusual, but there was a strategy behind it.

Many black individuals are familiar with receiving calls, especially from unknown numbers, and often associate such calls with overdue bills or inquiries from doctor's offices, among other things. Consequently, they might employ tactics to avoid speaking to a bill collector, such as pretending they are not at home.

However, when I made the calls, the recipients didn't immediately recognize it as a bill collection call because I adopted a friendly tone and didn't sound like the typical bill collector. Meaning, I didn't sound like a white person.

Of course, over time, those who were consistently late in their payments eventually realized that it was me calling, and some resorted to the same tactics they used with other bill collectors. It's worth noting that I also encountered situations where people I personally knew were on the receiving end of these calls.

In some cases, this led to confrontations, like the incident with a white girl from my school who became irate when I called her regarding her overdue bill. I suspect it upset her to know that not only was I the one making the call, but that I also had knowledge of her personal circumstances. As she might have perceived herself as superior to me, yet I was the one reaching out to her about her late payment.

That's the thing about small towns, everyone knew everyone. Therefore, I did know most of the people I was calling; and unfortunately, some were family and friends.

When I accepted the job, I didn't anticipate that I would be working as a bill collector. However, through this experience, I gained valuable insights into life and how individuals with lower incomes were treated and perceived.

We often contacted people who were one or two months behind on their bills and asked, "When can you pay your bill?" If they were unable to make the payment, we would offer alternatives such as refinancing their bill for another 24 months, providing them with $60.00, and allowing them to skip the next month's payment.

Unfortunately, more often than not, people would agree to these terms without considering that they were effectively extending their debt for an additional 24 months for only a small sum of money. However, given their circumstances, they felt they had no other choice.

Despite my initial belief that I was hired to fulfill a quota, I found that everyone I worked with was kind and I formed friendships with them all. While most of my colleagues were older than me, Sherry and Kim were closer to my age.

Sherry, who unlike Kim, was single so we began hanging out together in Valdosta. Lynn, who was my boss and attended school with my mom, was always warm and wore a constant smile.

Even after I quit the job after a year, not because I disliked it but because I needed higher earnings, I would return to visit them in the following years. I interviewed for a position at a company called Nashville Mills, which was located approximately 25 minutes east of Adel. Fortunately, I was offered the job.

Starting out, my hourly wage was around $9.25, a significant increase compared to the previous $5.00 per hour I earned. I was thrilled when I received my first paycheck and saw the difference. Around this time, Chris had graduated from high school and was preparing to attend technical school.

He also secured a job at Nashville Mills. My daily routine consisted of attending school in the morning in Valdosta, returning home to Adel, taking a nap, getting ready for work, picking up lunch/dinner, and then Chris and I would head to Nashville Mills for our shift from 3:00 p.m. to 11:00 p.m.

We followed this schedule five days a week. Occasionally, I would have to pick up my nephew from daycare and care for him between the 12:00 p.m. to 3:00 p.m. time slot. Dre, adored the character Barney, and we had bought him a videotape of the Barney show.

I would play the video for him and then doze off while he watched. When the video ended, he would wake me up, and I would rewind it, restart it, and go back to sleep. This became our routine.

Initially, I pursued a major in Political Science intending to attend law school. I viewed it as one of the many degrees I could obtain to embark on a law degree. However, when I discovered that I would need to take multiple math classes, I decided to switch my major to Legal Studies.

This major only required one math course, which still allowed me to pursue my goal of attending law school. I was overjoyed when I passed that one math class with a C. Regarding foreign language requirements, I took two French courses in high school and achieved good grades in both.

However, upon entering college, I was required to continue studying French at a higher level where the teacher exclusively spoke French. Although I only needed to take two French classes, I ended up taking it three times because I failed the first one with a D. While it may not have been considered a true failure, it felt like one to me.

During my time in college, there's a distinct

memory of visiting one of my high school teachers' homes for a particular reason, though the exact purpose escapes me now. It's possible my grandmother had asked me to pick something up, but the details are fuzzy. When I entered the house, I found another teacher from high school, someone who had actually been my instructor, sitting on the couch.

I greeted both of them, and the teacher asked me what I was doing after high school graduation. I replied, "I'm going to VSU," to which she inquired about my chosen major. I answered, "Legal Studies."

Her response to me has stayed with me and continues to agitate me to this day. She casually remarked, "Oh, so you'll be another black kid who can't find a job after graduation."

It's astonishing to think that a black teacher could make such a discouraging statement to a black student who was planning to attend law school. I can't recall exactly how I reacted, but I'm certain I didn't respond rudely because I would never be disrespectful to an adult. However, I was profoundly taken aback by her unkind comment.

Fortunately, I encountered the same teacher about three or four years later while she was eating at a McDonald's. She recognized me when I entered and greeted me as if she had never uttered those hurtful words.

I'm not entirely sure how I managed to seize the opportunity, but I conveyed something along the lines of, "Yes, I'm on my lunch break. I work across the street at a law firm as a paralegal." Simply making that statement brought me a great deal of satisfaction.

While she may not have connected the dots or realized how unkind she had been to me several years prior, it felt good to let her know that this young black woman had indeed secured employment in her field of study after college.

Once I reached my major-specific classes, everything went smoothly. I thoroughly enjoyed my legal studies courses. In one of my law classes, we had the opportunity to participate in a mock trial with our classmates.

Throughout the course, we developed the entire case and upon completion, we had the chance to present it at an actual courthouse. I even invited my family to attend and participate as witnesses in the case. It was an incredible experience, and I had the time of my life. At that moment, I knew that pursuing a career in law was the right path for me.

During my junior year of college, I encountered a scheduling conflict. There was a class I needed to take that was only offered in the evening, which meant I couldn't continue working my previous shift from 3:00 p.m. to 11:00 p.m. at Nashville Mills.

Determined to find a solution, I approached my boss and inquired about changing my schedule. As luck would have it, there was an opening on the third shift from 11:00 p.m. to 7:00 a.m., which I could temporarily take until the regular employee returned.

So, I transitioned to working nights while

attending evening classes. It was challenging, but I adapted and did what was necessary. This wasn't my first experience working night shifts, as I had done so in high school. On some weekends, I had worked overnight shifts at the Truck Stop from 11:00 p.m. to 7:00 a.m.

I managed to maintain this schedule for one semester before realizing that returning to my regular shift no longer aligned with my needs. Unfortunately, I still had evening classes that were required, so I made the difficult decision to quit.

During my time at college, I participated in work-study at Valdosta State University for a few hours each day. Additionally, I tried my hand at being a salesman for alarm systems, but it didn't pan out, and I quickly realized it wasn't the right fit for me.

My dear grandmother Almarie was one of the few individuals who purchased a system from me, and due to her fixed income, my Aunt Daisy put it in her name just to assist me in making a sale.

As I approached the end of my college journey, a requirement emerged for me to complete an internship in my chosen field. To facilitate this, my teacher, Dr. Ellerbee, reached out to a contact she knew. Dr. Ellerbee had transitioned from a legal career as a lawyer to become a professor, and her husband held a position as a Judge.

Thanks to her connections, I secured a position at a small attorney's office in Valdosta. However, my time there was brief, lasting only about a week before I was let go.

Yes, you heard that right – I was fired. It's important to note that this internship was unpaid, which may beg the question of how one can be fired from an unpaid position. Allow me to explain.

During my time there, a task arose involving the preparation and mailing of some discovery documents for a case. The paralegal had already assembled the discovery materials into a large envelope and labeled it. My sole responsibility was to drop it off at the post office and cover the postage expenses. Unfortunately, circumstances required the package to be repackaged and relabeled.

When I proceeded to update the label, I inadvertently reversed the address. As a result, the package was delivered back to our office instead of its intended destination within two or three days.

Understandably, the attorney was quite upset about the situation, and it's likely he may have viewed me as lacking competence, despite the mistake being relatively minor. I was rather nervous because it was within my first few days on the job, and I hadn't anticipated having to perform this particular task initially.

The attorney instructed his paralegal to terminate my internship, and he opted not to speak with me personally. This marked the first, but not the last, time I experienced being let go from a job.

My next internship opportunity arose at a small law firm in Valdosta called Copeland and Haugabrook, which primarily consisted of all African American professionals. I learned about this opportunity from my cousin Yumaka, who worked there as a paralegal. Having previously worked together at Nashville Mills, she put in a good word for me.

I was allowed to shadow a lady by the name of Mrs. Pat and assist with some typing tasks. I only worked a few hours a day in this capacity. At some point, the firm needed to hire someone for filing purposes. Seizing the opportunity, I proposed that I could handle the filing instead of them outsourcing the task, and in return, I would receive payment for my services.

This changed the dynamics of my job, but at least I was now earning a salary, although it was still relatively low given the time (1999). Similarly, to when I worked at First Franklin, the pay remained low. Fortunately, during this period, Chris continued working at Nashville Mills and was earning a decent income, allowing him to provide financial support.

Additionally, I was still living with my mom, so my major expenses were limited to my car, and I received quarterly refund checks from college loans. This allowed me to sustain myself for a while. Despite thinking that my boss was one of the meanest individuals I knew, I genuinely enjoyed working at the office. When he was present, we all felt on edge.

Our team comprised two black male law partners, two paralegals, a receptionist, me, and a female black law associate who joined later. Most of us worked for

Mr. Copeland, while Yumaka was the sole employee working for Mr. Haugabrook.

Yumaka cherished her work situation since her boss happened to be the nicer of the two. He possessed a gentle demeanor and spoke softly. Moreover, he was the epitome of impeccable dress, always sporting perfectly tailored suits.

On the other hand, Mr. Copeland was the complete opposite. He was loud and intimidating, often standing over Mrs. Pat, his paralegal, dictating what he wanted her to type. Just imagine having someone constantly looming over you while you type, taking dictation.

Mrs. Pat was skilled at her job and had been working for him for a long time, so she had grown accustomed to it. However, it was quite intimidating for me. Nevertheless, I am incredibly grateful for this opportunity as it allowed me to accumulate the necessary internship hours and gain valuable experience working in a legal office.

I learned the essential legal terminology and the importance of meeting deadlines, which are critical in the legal profession. Eventually, I made the decision to quit and become a full-time server at Shoney's during my last semester of college. I couldn't sustain myself on a meager weekly income of $100.

Chris and I got married on January 1, 2000, and I needed to earn more money to support our new life together. I approached Mr. Copeland and asked if I could work full-time, but unfortunately, he couldn't hire me full-time. Consequently, I had to seek employment elsewhere.

I'm sure you're wondering, "Wait a minute, go back a little and tell us about you and Chris getting married." Okay, okay. Chris and I had planned to marry three times before we tied the knot. The first time was in high school, and the second time was around a year or so into college.

During the second attempt, I had already purchased a wedding dress, ordered the cake, asked my bridesmaids to participate, and requested my stepdad, Rob, to walk me down the aisle.

My dad, who was not in prison at that time, was unhappy about this idea and expressed dissatisfaction openly. My family wasn't fans either but that's what I wanted. Yes Rob and mom's relationship ended badly, however as I got older I reestablished my relationship with him. Some people might not understand how that could be but he was the father that was there growing up, even if it was disfunctional. That's family right?

Also, my dad and I still didn't have a great relationship at this time. He was still in and out of some type of trouble due to his drug addiction, but we were at least talking. Not enough to want him to walk me down the aisle. I always looked at it as my dad didn't do anything worthy of having that right other than conceiving me, period.

All of this was arranged when Chris decided to call it off. I was devastated and couldn't believe it. I understand it and appreciate it now, but at the time, I was a 19-year-old young girl planning a wedding and my fiancé just cancelled it.

Now to be fair, he was devastated when I called it off in high school. He didn't understand why we still couldn't get married just because I decided not to go to the military.

And I didn't understand why he thought we should rush, now that we had more time. Unfortunately, we both had our hearts broken at some point during this engagement.

We even took a "break" during our 5-year dating stint. You remember when I said Chris and I were a little different? Our differences came full force when he felt I was too high maintenance. I was a girly girl who liked getting my hair and nails done and was a people person.

Chris had a hard time dealing with that. So, while he was in technical school, he met this young lady he was studying with and thought he had much more in common with than me.

Because we were having issues, I told him: let's take a break. I told him he could date the little girl he met, with whom he had so much in common with, and I would go hang out since neither had been single since we were 16. I started going to teen clubs on the weekend and hanging out with my brother's then girlfriend, who had the same name as me. We would go out Friday and Saturday night.

While I was going out, Chris was hanging out with this plain Jane chick he met at school. After two weeks of this, we decided it wasn't fun anymore and got back together. My mom was happy that we got back together because she hated the partying. It was only two weeks, but that wasn't me, so it bothered her.

Once we got back together, we were ready to get married but couldn't financially pay for a wedding. I was still in college and only working part-time. However, we found a way to solve this problem pretty quickly, though.

CHAPTER 14

In 1999, my mom was in a relationship with a man named Robert, and they had been planning to get married. They had been talking about it for quite some time and were ready to take the next step. That's when I came up with the idea of having a double wedding since Chris and I had been engaged for a long time but hadn't gotten married yet.

It seemed like a great plan to split the costs and make it a memorable event. We decided to set the date for January 1, 2000, which, as many people may remember, was a time of concern due to Y2K. There were worries that computer systems wouldn't handle the transition from 1999 to 2000, potentially causing problems worldwide.

Despite the concerns, we chose that day because I wanted to be one of the first people to get married in the new century, and having a double wedding added to the excitement. We made sure to announce the mother-daughter double wedding in the newspapers of the surrounding cities. It quickly became the talk of the town.

However, some people misunderstood the situation and assumed my mom was intruding on my wedding day, when actually it was me intruding on hers. We overheard comments like, "She should let that girl have her own special day." or "Why does she feel the need to get married at the same time as her daughter?"

But for the most part, it was good vibes. Due to the dynamics of the wedding, I no longer thought it was good idea for my first stepdad Rob, (yes both of my mom's husband's names are Robert), to walk me down the aisle.

I felt bad about this, but I had to respect the situation. Having my ex-stepdad give me away at my mom's wedding wouldn't look great. Therefore, we came up with a genius idea. My brother walked both of us down the aisle. He walked my mom down first, then returned to get me and walked me down the aisle.

It was a great wedding and reception. Nothing extravagant but simple and nice. My cousin Marcella was the wedding coordinator, my mom's friend Sherlene catered the party for free, and we hired a local photographer.

I remember standing outside, waiting for my brother to walk my mother into the church and come back to get me. Most brides are nervous or jittery, I was none of the above. I was super excited. I had been dating Chris for 5 years and I was ready to be his bride. The song I walked in on was, "You Are So Beautiful to Me" by Kenny Rogers.

After the wedding, Chris and I went home because we couldn't afford a honeymoon. Our home after we got married was a mobile home trailer owned by Chris' oldest sister Gwen. She had moved out years prior, leaving the trailer vacant. After discussing it with her, she agreed to let us rent it from her.

The trailer was a two-bedroom single-wide in a trailer park not far from where my mom still lived. However, shortly after we moved in, we discovered that due to the house being abandoned for a period of time and it having a small hole behind the stove, it was infested with rodents.

We would constantly see them scurrying around, which was quite unnerving as I have a strong fear of rats. We decided to set out rat traps, and to our surprise, we caught one after another. It became apparent that it was not that same rat but a series of them. After some investigation, that is when we discovered the hole.

We promptly sealed the hole, which put an end to the rodent problem. Nevertheless, living in the trailer had become less than ideal. After around nine months, we moved into a townhouse a few miles outside of town. It was a 2 bedroom, 2.5 bath townhome. We truly felt we had moved up then or at least made significant progress.

CHAPTER 15

I completed my BA in Legal Studies with a minor in Criminal Justice in June of 2000. Despite graduating, I was still working at Shoney's but had a strong desire to start my career in the legal field, preferably as a secretary or paralegal. Going to law school as planned immediately after college was no longer in my plans.

One reason is because I worked so much in high school, that my GPA wasn't as high as it needed to be to get into law school. I would have had to get a great score on the LSAT. Secondly, I didn't have the money to go. I would have had to get loans to pay for all of it, including room and board . Thirdly, it wasn't a law school in my town, so I would have to move to whereever I got accepted. Therefore, I decided to get a job as a paralegal first and go to law school later.

Atlanta had always been a city I wanted to move to, so I began my job search there. I applied online through a temp agency, and they invited me for a typing test and an interview. Unfortunately, nothing came of it as they kept emphasizing that I needed prior experience, which seemed like a catch-22 situation to me. How could I gain experience if no one was willing to hire me?

Feeling disheartened, I decided to revisit

Copeland and Haugabrook to inquire about job opportunities. I had an interview with Mrs. Walker, who offered me a position but at a meager wage of around $6.50 per hour.

Being offered such a low salary after earning a degree was frustrating. This experience left me feeling discouraged, especially since I continued working at Shoney's for another nine months after graduating from college.

It's a common misconception among college students that job opportunities will simply fall into their laps upon graduation. Unfortunately, the reality is different but with patience in time, you will get a job.

While I enjoyed my time as a server, it was starting to wear on me. I despised how some people would look down on servers, thinking they were superior. I would often vent my frustrations to my coworker and friend Nilay, expressing how it angered me, especially considering that I knew I was more educated than many of the patrons who held such attitudes.

After a prolonged period of searching, I eventually landed a job at a law firm specializing in bankruptcy cases. I served as a receptionist there for approximately five months before I found myself being let go once more. This second job loss was a significant blow to my self-esteem. Within the span of just two years, I had experienced two job terminations in my chosen field.

Subsequently, I faced a distressing two-month period of unemployment. This situation was particularly agonizing for me, as I hadn't been without a job since the age of 16. The absence of a steady income during that time was truly devastating for me.

I frequently advise young individuals to be aware that there's a possibility of being fired from their first job after college, primarily because they might not have the necessary skills to perform the job effectively. It's important to understand that while school helps you graduate, it doesn't necessarily prepare you for the specific demands of a job.

Practical experience is the true teacher when it comes to mastering a role. Armed with this understanding, I urge them not to allow such an experience to devastate them, as it did to me when it happened. It's a part of life's journey.

However, I soon gained employment at Clyatt, Clyatt, and Golden, a law firm operated by a husband-and-wife team. The firm consisted of three white partners and an aspiring black attorney named Tabitha Ponder. I was hired as a secretary, specifically for Robert Clyatt, the husband.

While I appreciated the opportunity, I couldn't help but feel a tad disappointed that I wasn't employed as a paralegal. Nevertheless, my compensation was higher than what I would have earned at another firm in a paralegal role.

However, I encountered difficulties with dictation, which involved Mr. Clyatt speaking into a recorder for me to transcribe, proofread, and present the documents for his review. As the weeks passed, I noticed his growing frustration, which instilled a fear of losing my job. Wanting to address the issue proactively, I approached him privately and honestly explained my struggles.

I assured him that I was giving my best effort and requested additional time to improve. Fortunately, he was open to working with me, and we devised a solution together.

I discovered that if I typed the dictated letters and revisited them later for proofreading, I could identify errors I had previously missed. By reading the text on paper rather than relying solely on my memory of the dictation, I significantly improved the quality of my work. This technique became my mastery, and it greatly enhanced my performance in the role.

I developed strong connections with my colleagues at the law firm, and our bond grew so tight that we became like a family. Tabitha, who successfully passed the bar exam, proved to be an incredible source of support and offered me invaluable assistance. As a result, I began working closely with her and eventually transitioned into the role of her paralegal.

Her mentorship was truly priceless, and I will forever be grateful for the knowledge I gained under her guidance. We would go out to lunch and she would expose me to foods that I didn't normally eat and encourage me to be open to new things.

Daysha, another secretary and a fellow alum of VSU, quickly became a close companion. We shared common acquaintances and formed a special bond. Alongside Daysha, I cherished the presence of Tracey, Rebecca, and Lisa, who were also paralegals within our team. Their camaraderie and shared experiences made our work environment even more fulfilling.

After approximately a year, Faith joined our team as a paralegal. Initially, I felt a tinge of frustration that she was hired instead of me being promoted from my role as a secretary. I hadn't started working as Tabitha's paralegal at that time.

However, any initial reservations quickly faded away, and we became fast friends, despite the age difference of 10 years. Our shared determination and drive brought us together, fostering a strong connection and mutual support.

CHAPTER 16

After being married for a year and a half, Chris and I wanted to conceive. We felt we were ready to have a baby, so I stopped taking the birth control pills that I had been taking for years. No one ever mentions that conceiving a kid is not as easy as just stopping taking birth control pills and then having sex all the time.

My parents had no problems conceiving and they weren't even trying. Along with so many girls in my community who again weren't trying to get pregnant and were able to have multiple babies with ease. So for us to have such a hard time was disheartening to say the least.

We tried consistently for months with no luck. Unfortunately, because I was no longer taking birth control pills, I was eventually diagnosed with endometriosis, a condition where tissue similar to the womb's lining grows in other places, such as the ovaries and fallopian tubes.

I used to have painful periods before, so I didn't think anything of it. It was just the price I had to pay to conceive but this condition caused me to have to undergo surgery to remove the excess tissues. It was outpatient surgery, and I was able to go back to work soon afterwards.

However, it happened again, and another surgery was required about a year later. At this point I'm just baffled. The doctor assured us this is not unusual and that we still could get pregnant. This condition just made it a little bit harder.

People kept asking, "When are you guys going have a baby?" It was so stressful and aggravating to me. To want something so bad, couldn't have it and then have everyone asking when are you going to have it, like it was totally up to me and Chris. Finally, I'm like, something else must be wrong. Let's schedule an appointment with my OBGYN, Dr. Taylor, for a full checkup.

Our first appointment was in November 2002. We went in and had a test and blood run to see if I was the problem. After getting the results back, we found out it wasn't me.

I was relieved, but it still didn't explain why I hadn't gotten pregnant. People kept saying, "You need to stop thinking about it and then it'll happen." Everyone wanted to give their unsolicited advice but I wanted advice from the professionals. So, they scheduled us an appointment to check Chris out to see if he was the problem.

Since it was close to the holidays, we were scheduled to go in January for the appointment. It was a waiting game until then. On New Year's Eve my Uncle Tony and Aunt Almaree had a party and Chris and I attended it. My Cousin Deborah was there along with other family members.

I remember her saying to me, "You're glowing. Are you pregnant?" I was like, "I wish, but no, I'm not." She said, "Well, you are definitely glowing." The day of the appointment, we were both ready to find out what was wrong and hopefully what can be done to help us conceive.

When we went in, they wanted to give me a pregnancy test just for fun before discussing Chris. We thought this was a waste of time, but hey, whatever. When the nurse came back in, she said, "You're pregnant!" We looked at her like she was crazy.

We couldn't believe it! We were over the moon with excitement. What were the odds of us going to get Chris tested to see why we couldn't get pregnant to find out that we were pregnant.

Chris couldn't wait to tell my mom. He knew she was ready for me to have a baby and was going to be thrilled to hear the news. He didn't even let me get it out of my mouth before he told her. Everyone around us was excited about the pregnancy.

When I say I loved being pregnant, believe me I loved being pregnant. Everyone treated me like a queen. They cooked me food, made sure I was comfortable, and opened doors for me. I got so much attention being pregnant that I was looking forward to baby number two. Chris and I talked about names and once we found out it was a boy, we decided on Thomas Christopher Woods.

He had my maiden name and his father's first name as his middle name. I wasn't a believer of Jr.'s. I wanted him to have his own identity. You never know, his dad could become an ax murderer, and now he has to live with this name.

I guess I felt like that because my dad was not a reputable person in the community. If my brother had been a junior, people might have judged him by his name. So, Thomas Christopher it was.

His name also reminded me of Christopher Robin on Winnie the Pooh so I decorated his room in Winnie the Pooh. Oh, how I loved decorating his room. He had his own baby crib, bassinet, tv, rocking chair and Winnie the Pooh stickers on the wall. I couldn't wait for him to arrive.

Thomas was scheduled to arrive on September 27, I believe, so I had it all scheduled in my head. I would work up to Sept 12th. That would give me a week to clean my house and do all the last-minute things I needed to do. Then I was going to take some Castor Oil on the 19th and go walking so I can have him on time or early.

My mom said she did this with one of us, so I was going to do it too because I was ready for him to arrive and definitely didn't want him to be later than September 27. But who knows that things don't ever go as planned.

I woke up Friday morning September 5th feeling as if I was peeing on myself. I ran to the bathroom to sit on the toilet. When I sat down, the peeing stopped. I sat there for a few minutes and then went back to get in the bed. I started peeing again. I was like, "OMG. I cannot stop peeing." So, I told Chris to give me the phone so I can call my nurse.

As I was explaining to her that I couldn't stop peeing but every time I sat on the toilet it stopped, she just started laughing at me. I'm like what's so funny. She was like, "Your water broke. Every time you sit on the toilet, the baby's head stops the flow. Come on into the hospital."

Now, this is my first child, so of course, this didn't occur to me at all. We rushed to get me ready and drove to the hospital. Once we got there, we discovered that my water broke but I hadn't dilated much. We still had a long way to go. We called everyone, but no one was there at that time but Chris and me.

Chris mentioned to me that he needed to call his teacher because he had a test that day. He had started back taking classes at Wire Grass Technical College. I told him to go to class. It was right down the road, and I wasn't having the baby any time soon, so he'll be back before anything happens. After persisting, he left only to return probably 20 minutes later. Once he told his teacher his wife was having a baby, he immediately sent him back to the hospital.

My mom, Aunt Debra and my friend Faith came to the hospital and stayed most of the night. Mr. Thomas did not want to come. Contractions were coming all day and evening, until I got to a point where I said, just take him.

Give me a c-section and get it over with. The doctors, nurse and my mom talked me out of it because the healing process of a c-section is so much longer than regular birth. The doctor discontinued the medication that had been used to initiate my delivery, which had been causing the contractions, and opted to allow me to rest for a period.

At about 3 or 4 in the morning, they returned and gave me an epidural to help me with the pain, and they started the contractions again. Thomas still didn't come into this world until Saturday at 12:06 p.m. That was the beginning of him doing things on his own time.

Thomas was a happy baby, and everyone loved him. I had prayed when I was pregnant with him that he be a happy jolly baby. I didn't want him to be one of those babies that cried every time someone wanted to hold him. God answered my prayers.

He was born 3 weeks after his twin cousins, so my mom had three new grandbabies within a month. On that note, I always thought that by the time I had a child, my child would get all the attention because he's my first child. But noooo, my brother and sister-in-law stole my shine by having the first girl and two of them at that.

I joke with them all the time, that they couldn't just let me have my moment. My brother played with the names of his kids a little like I did. He wanted to have his name in it somehow. My nephew is named Vanico after my brother, and the twin girls are called Vanica and Shanica.

While I was pregnant, I reconnected with two

of my classmates who were also pregnant. Shayla and Keesha became my pregnant buddies. We were able to talk about what we were going through as pregnant women as it was all three of our first time having a baby. We hung out all the time.

All our babies were due at different times. Shayla was due in the summer; I was due in September and Keesha was due in December. After all the babies were born, we continued to hang out and have play dates for the kids. Having them was definitely a God send to me. Especially after things started changing with Chris and I.

CHAPTER 17

When people say that kids change things, they're not lying. Chris and I definitely changed after Thomas. He started getting more distance and I started being consumed with taking care of Thomas.

I wanted to be the best mother to him and tried my best to do everything right. When he slept, I slept so that I could spend time with him when he was up. I stayed off for 10 weeks with him and when I returned back to work, I only went back part time for a while.

I didn't want him to stay in the daycare, more than he spent time with me. Chris started working later and more often during this time. It was Thomas and I most of the time. I kept asking him what was wrong, but he always said nothing. Things were getting more strained, and we were arguing more.

I felt that it was someone else, but I couldn't prove it. At this time, we were staying in a home across from my mother's home and our electricity was outrageous. We needed to find another rental to live in so my then boss had a daughter who was moving out of her home and wanted to rent it, so I had made arrangements for us to move.

Prior to us moving, the heat went out in the home we were still living in and it was in the middle of the winter. I told Chris that I was going to stay with my mom until we moved because it was too cold for us to stay there with Thomas and of course he was welcome to come. Because we weren't in a good place, he decided not to. As we say, this was the beginning of the end.

Several days later, when it was time to move to the new home, we packed up the U-Haul and moved all the furniture to the new house. However, after everything was moved in, Chris advised me that he wasn't moving in. I felt like someone had punched me in the stomach.

I was shocked and devastated. Like where do we do that at, and make this make sense? He tried to convince me he felt abandoned when we left to stay with my mom and that we agreed to never leave each other. Of course, to me, this was completely asinine.

I didn't leave because of our issues, but because Thomas couldn't stay in that cold ass house. He was truly reaching. After some back and forth, I had to let it go. I couldn't force him to stay with his family. At some point, Chris decided he needed to be with his family, and he moved back in.

However, things didn't get better. He was always "working", never home in the afternoon and more and more distant, and not just to me but to our family as a whole. Thomas is truly a mommy's boy because he spent all his time with me in his early years.

Rumors were coming back to me that Chris was cheating or that he was seeing someone, but no one gave me concrete proof until one day. A friend of the family told me that his truck had been spotted a lot in some subdivision called something Park. I cannot remember the actual name of it now, but I do know that it had the word Park in it.

Now he had been telling me that he was stressed out at work because of all the long hours, and that he would sometimes go to sit at the park at night to get his mind right. That was ludicrous to me, but I wanted to give him the benefit of the doubt.

At some point, I would ride around the "parks" in the area to see if he was indeed at the park. Of course, I never found him. When I heard about the subdivision called this, I was like, okay, cool. One night on my way home, I decided to ride through the subdivision. Thomas was in the back seat sleeping in his car seat.

He was about 16 months at this time. Now before you think, I should never have had my son in the car, just listen to the rest of the story. As I was riding around, low and behold, I saw Chris' truck backed into someone's yard like he lived there! I was like OMG really? I blew my horn and stayed in my car.

Next, I saw a female moving the curtains back to see who was blowing the horn. Also, I just blew the horn once. I wasn't blaring on it or anything. I was very civilized. About 2 minutes later, Chris comes outside and bends down to look in the window.

He looks at me and then Thomas in the back seat and says to me, "I'll be home in a minute." I responded, "Yes, you do that." and I left. In hindsight, I should have waited until he got in his truck and followed him home but unfortunately, I didn't.

I drove home, put Thomas in bed, and went to the kitchen. I calmly got as many trash bags as possible and proceeded to go to the closet and pack his bags. I was not in a hurry, I took my time, and did it very calmly. This was not going to be a *Waiting to Exhale* scene I promise.

By the time I was done, Chris still wasn't home. Now I'm pissed off. Before, I was like, 'Thank God I'm not crazy". But NOW, I'm like, this is how you are going to play me. I called Faith, who lived nearby, and asked her if she could come sit with Thomas for me because now, I'm about to show my ass.

She readily agreed and came within 10 minutes. I told her, if Chris comes while I'm gone, just leave once he gets there. I rode back to where I had found him earlier, but his truck was gone this time.

As I drove back to the house, I called his mother. I asked her if she had spoken with Chris, and she said no. I asked her to tell him to come pick up his clothes if she spoke with him.

She was like "Um... okay." Since she didn't ask me any questions, I figured she already knew or didn't want to get involved. However, I'm assuming I was the last person to know.

Faith called me when I was almost home and told me that Chris was home and that she had left. I could hear sympathy in her voice. She said she walked out as he walked in and said hi and bye on the way home.

Chris asked her where I was and she told him that I was on my way. When I walked in, Chris had his story ready. He was at his cousin's house and the girl that looked out the window was his cousin's girlfriend and that there was nothing to what I just saw.

If that was all true, he shouldn't have had any problem taking me back to meet his cousin and girlfriend. He wanted to convince me that it was too late to return to these people's house and that I should trust him.

At this point, I truly feel that if he had just admitted he made a mistake and told me what he had done, we MIGHT would not have gone through all that we went through after this, but he didn't. He continued to attempt to make me think that I was crazy and that it was just me.

The end of this conversation resulted in Chris taking all his clothes and leaving that night. I don't think I've ever slept so well that first night. The weight of "not knowing" had been lifted. There had been signs over the past year, but they all made sense now.

The explanations I accepted for those signs couldn't be accepted anymore. I remember one night walking in on him in the middle of the night in the guest room and it looked as though he was holding something that looked like it could be a phone, but he convinced me that it wasn't.

Another sign was when I bought him a book I thought he would like for Christmas but didn't realize he already had the book. Now, Chris is not a reader and would never buy it for himself, but I thought, okay, maybe he got it from someone. Well, he did get it from someone else, his new lady friend. He even brought a toy to our son from his side chic and I didn't realize it until after all was said and done.

Things like this happened that I knew didn't feel right, but I couldn't pinpoint the truth. So, to know the truth and to know that I wasn't just imagining things was such a relief.

Over the next couple of months, I actually fought to keep my marriage together even after the infidelity, but the funny thing was, Chris didn't want to make it work.

He was so wrapped up in his new life. He spoke with me several days later and gave me some of the truth I needed, but he kept a lot of it from me. His betrayal was the most devastating thing I thought could happen to me at that time. I felt like, "God why me? I did everything right didn't I?"

I graduated high school, went to college, got married before having my son, never got into trouble and helped anyone who needed me. I felt I did everything in order in God's eyes. Why did this happen to me? However, I'm sure if Chris told his version of this, he would probably say that he felt neglected after Thomas was born. Not that it justifies it but I'm sure he felt this way.

Chris and I never wanted our kid to go through what we went through growing up. Chris and his twin sister were the babies out of seven kids and his mom was also a single mother. His dad wasn't in his life as much as he would have liked, and we vowed to never allow that to happen to any kids we might have. Unfortunately, no matter good intentions, some things are out of your control.

Chris had eventually gotten his own apartment at this time, and we were co-parenting. He continued to take care of Thomas and helped pay some of the bills in the house. We became legally separated while trying to make this work as amicable as we could.

I started talking to someone else at this time. I figured, why not? Funny thing, I was waiting to meet Chris at an ATM to give me some money for Thomas when a guy pulled up beside me.

I thought it was Chris for a minute because he was short with the same complexion as him. The guy walked to the ATM and then he came back. I was sitting in the car waiting for Chris, when the guy, asked me what my name was. We started a conversation and was in the middle of it when Chris pulled up. He tried to act unbothered, but of course he was.

There was a lot of back and forth after the initial break up, but it just couldn't work. Every time we tried; I believe only one of us was trying. Either he was trying, and I was over it and still interested in someone else, or I was trying, and he wasn't and still interested in someone else. We went through unnecessary financial hardship because Chris lost his job.

The young lady he was cheating with worked at his job and unfortunately, that didn't end well. He was bouncing around from job to job making me the sole provider in between time. I was resentful and angry.

I had lost the unconditional love I always had for him. We had previously experienced financial issues, from time to time, some from us being young, me being unemployed, others due to Chris overspending, or when Chris was not working due to some medical issues.

We had a car repossessed and even had to file for bankruptcy at one point, but I loved my husband and was in it for the long haul. However, when the unconditional love was gone, everything he did got on my nerves. Especially when I felt like he caused all these unnecessary issues along with breaking my heart.

I must admit that we did make efforts, but ultimately, that's all we could do. I recall a moment in church during one of our breakup periods when the pastor was delivering a sermon about the vows of marriage, emphasizing the commitment through thick and thin, in sickness and in health, and all the traditional wedding vows.

It stirred a sense of sadness within me and rekindled the desire to give it another try, which I did. However, my heart wasn't fully invested in it anymore. Despite Chris' strong desire to make things work, I couldn't. In the end, I found solace in knowing that I had exhausted every possible effort.

Finally, we called it quits for the last time and had to tell our then three-year-old that we were divorcing. We sat him on the bed and told him that mommy and daddy weren't going to live together anymore.

I'm not sure how much of the conversation he truly understood at that young age, but it broke my heart to see him crying like he understood every word. I will say, looking back it now, that we were just too young.

We started dating at sixteen and was in a committed relationship until we got married at twenty-one and then it was death do us part. Many couples can marry their high school sweetheart and live happily after all but it's not without some hurdles and challenges.

But I feel that we didn't have time to explore dating and being young without having the burden of being in a committed relationship. If we had gotten dating out of our system during high school and college, we might have been more settled by the time we decided to get married, but we weren't.

And unfortunately, we couldn't withstand the hurdles and challenges we had to endure. Chris is a great guy who just wasn't ready for a wife and child, and we didn't learn that until after it was too late. But I know that everything that happened was supposed to happen because it produced my son and helped me to get where I am today.

CHAPTER 18

By 2006, I had reached a point of deep dissatisfaction with my job, my pursuit of a teaching degree, and life in general in South Georgia. I was thoroughly fed up, and I decided to take action.

There were a couple of individuals who played a pivotal role in pushing me to this breaking point, and two of them were my aunt and uncle. I vividly recall a day when I was at my Aunt Daisy and Uncle Larry's house, and they suggested that I should seriously consider joining the Air Force.

They believed it could be a fantastic opportunity for me, especially given that I already had a degree, which would allow me to enter as an officer. This, they reasoned, would provide financial stability and the flexibility to care for Thomas, particularly when he fell ill—an important consideration, especially since I was suffering with sinus issues at the time and lacked healthcare coverage through my job.

While they genuinely believed that joining the Air Force was a brilliant idea, I found myself extremely disturbed by their suggestion, and here's why. I felt that I had already earned a four-year degree and was working at a law firm part time. Furthermore, I had started attending VSU again to obtain a master's degree in special education, with the goal of becoming a teacher to improve my circumstances and provide my son with the essential medical insurance he required.

Additionally, I aspired to have the freedom to be with him during the summers. Despite all of this, it seemed that their expectations were still beyond what I was already striving to achieve.

I was confused. Nonetheless, from their perspective, it appeared as though I had pursued all these avenues, yet my situation remained unsatisfactory, leading them to believe that perhaps I needed to explore a different path.

Another person who helped me make my decision was an attorney by the name of Mike Ryder. He worked at a law firm in Atlanta called Swift, Currie, McGhee, & Hiers.

Our office worked with him on a lot of cases, and he used to call me to get information because my boss wasn't very cooperative. He loved working with me but hated working with my office. He would casually say, "If you ever want to move to Atlanta, I got a job for you." He said it all the time, and I would just laugh it off.

But one day I started thinking seriously about it after speaking with someone that I had met who lived in Atlanta. While speaking with him, he was a teacher himself, I was sharing my aunt and uncle's advice and explaining that I was pursuing a teaching degree with the aim of having summers off, spending afternoons with my son and having good healthcare.

It was at this point that he imparted wisdom that

altered the course of my life. He said, "If your desire to attend school to become a teacher stems from a genuine love for teaching, then by all means, continue down that path.

However, if your motivation is primarily to have summers off and evenings free, it's worth reconsidering. If you truly enjoy what you do, there are alternative ways to pursue it." That was the moment when I took all three of those conversations and made my decision to do something different.

This was during the Christmas holiday weekend so I couldn't reach out at that time, but as soon as the new year came around, I reached out to Mike Ryer. I told him that I wanted to move to Atlanta and wanted to know if he had a job for me.

He said yes. He would have HR give me a call to schedule an interview. I was elated. I couldn't want. Janie in HR called me that same week and scheduled an interview.

I worked with other offices in Atlanta, so on a call with Kesha Kennedy, a secretary at Drew, Eckl & Farnahm, I mentioned that I was coming up that way for an interview.

Unbeknownst to me, these two companies were competitors, so she immediately said, "You need to interview with us also." I thought this was hilarious but she was serious. She had a conversation with her supervisor, who then relayed the message to the HR department.

Before I knew it, I had secured two interview

appointments in Atlanta. I was overjoyed. The likelihood of transitioning from having no interviews to suddenly having two, all within the span of a week or so, was incredible.

Why this was so surprising to me is because when I first graduated from college, I applied and interviewed with several temp agencies to work as a paralegal but unfortunately, everyone kept saying I needed experience.

This was discouraging and heartbreaking to me at the time because how could I get experience if no one would hire me? So having the opportunity to interview with 2 top firms without going through a temp agency was rare for Atlanta.

Mostly all firms in Atlanta hire their employees from temp agencies. The old saying that "It isn't what you know but who you know." was so true. If I hadn't known Mike Ryder or Kesha Kennedy, I definitely would not have gotten this opportunity.

On the day of my interview with Swift, Currie, McGhee & Hiers my friend Nilay and I drove up there for it. I remember having micro braids in my hair and wearing a loud pink pantsuit that I thought looked great on me.

Too bad I didn't realize that blue, black, and gray are the best interview colors for a professional interview. When I walked in, they took me to a conference room to wait on Janie.

When she came in and introduced herself, I learned that they were interviewing for an attorney named Briggs Peery. I was a little surprised because I thought I would be working for Mike Ryder but I wasn't.

The interview went awesome. Janie asked me what I was looking for as salary and because I didn't know what the going salary was, I gave her a salary amount that I thought was fair. She said, " OKAY" and that she would let me know in a week or so.

Two days later I came back up to an interview with Drew Eckl & Farnham. To be honest, I really don't recall how that interview went. I just remember Nico and my mom driving me up and waiting on me to interview.

All of this was in the 2nd week of January. I heard back from Swift Currie first that I had the job if I wanted it. I wanted to hear back from Drew Eckl before making a decision, so I called to check in with them.

They said they hadn't decided yet. Therefore, I went with Swift Currie. I wasn't going to lose my opportunity waiting on them. I was going to start work on February 1st with a starting salary $10,000 more than I asked for. This was a miracle and I felt truly blessed.

I was the only one who was excited. Well maybe not the only one. However, my mom was devastated. Even though she knew I was interviewing, when I officially got the job and said I was going she was heartbroken. Prior to this time, my mom had several health problems.

She had been in a car accident and injured her

back and she had undergone open heart surgery. I was there to take care of her during both times. However, after her heart surgery she started thinking her life was over. She felt she would never work again, and my mom was only 45 years old during the time of her surgery.

During this period, my son and I (Chris and I were separated) made the decision to leave the rental house I had been leasing from my boss's daughter and we moved in with my mom to provide her with assistance. Over time, she had become increasingly reliant on me and started believing that she couldn't manage things independently, despite her doctor's assurance that she could resume working.

I did my best to motivate and support her, but she was resistant to my advice. When I eventually made the choice to relocate to Atlanta, she interpreted it as abandonment. In my perspective, however, the move was aimed at improving the quality of life for both my son and me, and it would enable me to offer her more financial assistance from Atlanta than I could while residing in Adel.

At that time, I was working part time at Clyatt, Clyatt & Golden making about $260 a week while going to school to be a Special Education teacher, that wasn't my calling. Something had to change. So, I broke my mother's heart and moved to Atlanta.

Chris wasn't particularly enthusiastic about this decision either. He had always held onto the hope of us reconciling, believing that our separation was merely a temporary break. Although he expressed a desire to move to Atlanta with us, it wasn't part of my plan.

The last breakup had marked the end of the road for me. I felt that I had exhausted all possibilities and that it was time for me to move forward. While my friends were saddened by the situation, they also recognized that it was the best course of action for me.

My boss attempted to persuade me to stay by offering more money, a new computer, and a few other incentives that escape my memory. However, my decision was unwavering. Perhaps if these offers had come before I had alternative options, I might have reconsidered, but once the opportunity in Atlanta presented itself, I couldn't turn back.

I was absolutely determined to make this move for the betterment of both myself and my son. One of my friends once told me, "Even if a meteorite were to land smack in the middle of your path to Atlanta, you'd find another way to get there." They were absolutely right!

Atlanta represented a fresh start for me and Thomas, filled with opportunities that could potentially transform our life. I was now a 28 year old divorced mother of a 3 year old son heading to a city where I didn't know anyone. This was exciting and scary but I went in with my eyes wide open, ready to embrace all that Atlanta had for us.

KIZZIE CRAWFORD

EPILOGUE

As I sit in the Virgin Atlantic Clubhouse in Johannesburg, South Africa watching my now husband play on his cell phone, I think about how far I've come.

We had just celebrated our 14-year wedding anniversary in Johannesburg and Cape Town for 10 days and were on our way back home. Who knew a little girl from Adel, GA could have made such a life for herself.

Moving to Atlanta 16 ½ years ago was the best thing I could have ever done. I met my current husband, who ironically is named Thomas just like my son and is from the same hometown, only 9 months after moving to Atlanta. Our mothers live around the corner from each other to this day.

Ironically, I asked him out for our first date, which was on his birthday. Two mutual friends introduced us, and we became an item quickly. We got married a year and half after meeting each other.

He is 6 ½ years older than me and had been in Atlanta 10 years prior to me. Together we have built a very successful life together. Thomas has owned a successful moving company for the last 17 years by the name Tate The Great Moving Company. His office is based out of Douglasville, GA.

Soon after moving to Atlanta, I obtained my MBA from the University of Phoenix that I didn't use until I started my real estate business about 6 years ago. After being in the legal field for 18 years, I decided I needed a change. I wanted to have my own business and be the boss I always knew I could be. Since then, I have built quite a name for myself in the real estate world.

I got my Broker license 3 years ago and continue to work with Keller Williams Realty Atlanta Partners in Peachtree City, Georgia. I've been in the top 5% of the office, I mentor other agents and serve on the Agent Leadership Council. I'm the KW Cultural Ambassador and teach Dual Career Courses along with holding other titles in the office.

I started a non-profit organization in 2016 by the name of Distinguished Young Ladies, Inc. We mentor middle and high school girls in Fulon County and surrounding counties in the community. My leaders, who are mostly my friends, and I have had numerous girls go through our program and we feel that we have truly made in impact in some of their lives.

Immediately after moving to Atlanta, I started making long lasting relationships with ladies that soon became my village. With me being in Atlanta with no family or friends, this was important to me. Some of the ladies that I met have been almost like sisters to me since I never had any.

Monique was one of the first person I met at my job who had a daughter the same age as my son. We became fast friends and did almost everything together. Some of the main things were taking our kids to Chuck E Cheese at least once a week. We loved it as much as they did. Monique showed me around Atlanta and for that I will be forever thankful.

Soon I found more girlfriends that either had kids that went to school or played sports with my son. All my friends had kids the same age as my son and now, most of us are empty nesters.

We frequently get together now to have "Book Club" meetings which are just "Cocktails and Conversations". We may talk about a book we read, or we might not

Allison and Nikki each are friends that came into my lives with boys the same age as Thomas. Their boys grew up with Thomas as if they were his brothers. They went to some of the same schools, participated in boy's scouts, sports and clubs together since they were about 6 years old until now.

My son Thomas, who we affectionately call King now, is almost 20 years old and starting his second year at Georgia State University. Before leaving from South Africa, we helped him move into his first apartment in the city of Atlanta.

He studied abroad this summer in London and had an awesome time. Once I married Thomas, I gained my bonus son Brice, and ironically enough we became fast friends.

He is 26 turning 27 soon. He and I always had a great relationship and never had any conflicts. He is now working at his dad's moving company and has his own apartment as well near Atlanta. Both boys have grown up to be such responsible young men and we are so proud of them.

Thomas and I are officially empty nesters and living our best lives now. We love to travel and make it a regular event in our lives. We took a trip to Mexico in January for 30 days because we wanted to get away from the cold weather in Atlanta.

Our anniversaries are always made a big deal. For our tenth year, we went to Paris and Italy which was wonderful, but I have to admit, South African has beat them all out. We had a great time visiting where our ancestors originated from and learning their history. I recommend everyone who can take a trip there one day.

We also love going out to dinner and attending networking events for our businesses on a regular basis. We recently sold our last home in Douglasville and bought our dream home about an hour outside of the city.

We are real estate investors who own several homes in Valdosta, Georgia and looking forward to purchasing more. We have currently started a YouTube channel, The Crawford Chronicles, and looking forward to seeing what happens with that. We are always looking at ways to enhance and build our legacy to leave to our kids and their kids.

My mom is still in Adel, and she is doing well. She went back to work after I left but eventually, I was able to help to retire her 10 years later. My brother and his family currently live in metro Atlanta about an hour or so from me. I was excited when he moved here and hopefully, we will encourage our mother to move here as well.

Leaving Adel 16 ½ years ago was the best decision I could have ever made. It gave me and my son opportunities that we never would have gained back home. Living in a city where you see so many successful people that look like you changes your perspective on life. It opens your eyes to all the possibilities that is out there.

It motivates you to work hard and believe that the world is limitless. We look forward to seeing what God has planned for us next. We are excited about the future.

Thank you for your support.

For speaking engagement inquiries for the author, please contact me directly at

authorkizziecrawford@gmail.com
www.authorkizziecrawford.com

For Kizzie Distinguished Realty, LLC
Business Related Queries Only
Tel: 1-404-907-9969

Printed in the United States of America
Paperback: ISBN: 9798859671397

Made in the USA
Columbia, SC
16 November 2023